Conversations with Gorbachev

MIKHAIL GORBACHEV—ZDENĚK MLYNÁŘ

Conversations
with
Gorbachev

ON PERESTROIKA, THE PRAGUE SPRING, AND
THE CROSSROADS OF SOCIALISM

Translated by George Shriver

COLUMBIA UNIVERSITY PRESS   NEW YORK

Columbia University Press
Publishers Since 1893
New York   Chichester, West Sussex

Copyright © 2002 Mikhail Gorbachev

Library of Congress Cataloging-in-Publication Data

Gorbachev, Mikhail Sergeevich, 1931-
Conversations with Gorbachev : on perestroika, the Prague
Spring, and the crossroads of socialism / Mikhail
Gorbachev, Zdenek Mlynar.
p. cm.
ISBN 0-231-11864-3 (cl.)
1. Gorbachev, Mikhail Sergeevich, 1931—Interviews.
2. Mlynâé, Zdenék—Interviews. 3. Perestroæka.
4. Czechoslovakia—History—Intervention, 1968.
5. Socialism. I. Mlynár, Zdenek. II. Title.

DK290.3.G67 A5 2002
943.704—dc21
2001058228

Columbia University Press books are printed on permanent
and durable acid-free paper.
Printed in the United States of America
c 10 9 8 7 6 5 4 3 2 1

PUBLISHER'S NOTE

Although a Russian edition of this book was planned, as of
this edition, no Russian edition exists. An edition was
published in Czech under the title *Reformatory nebyvaji
stastni. Dialog o "perestrojce," Prazskem jaru a socialismu.*
It was published by the Victoria publishing house, Prague,
in 1995.

CONTENTS

by Archie Brown

This book, based on conversations between Mikhail Gorbachev and the late Zdeněk Mlynář, is an important historical document. It provides insights into the evolution of the political ideas of two highly intelligent people—from dogmatic Communism to Communist reformism (or revisionism) to a social democratic understanding of socialism. When one of those concerned played the decisive role in the pluralization of Soviet politics and in the ending of Soviet domination of Eastern Europe, that gives an especial significance to how his way of looking at the world gradually evolved.

There are critics of Gorbachev who have denied that his ideas shifted fundamentally on the grounds that he continued to express a commitment to "socialism." Such criticism represents an all too common failure to understand the gulf separating the "socialism" of orthodox Communism, based on Marxist-Leninist ideology and the monopoly of power of a highly disciplined ruling party, from the "socialism" espoused by West European mass parties that throughout the greater part of the twentieth century competed, generally successfully, with Communists for the support of working-class and many middle-class voters.

A misunderstanding of social democracy is widespread both in Russia and the United States, for neither country—unlike the majority of European (especially West European) states—has had a successful social democratic movement or party. During the perestroika period the late Alec Nove drew attention to the growing number of ideologues of the market economy to be found in Russia who had taken to "denouncing the West European welfare state in the crudest Chicago terms" and who "seem to see not only Swedes but even the West German social democrats as dangerous lefties who desire to travel the road to serfdom *slowly*."[1] In reality, the attachment of West European social democrats to liberty stands up to scrutiny at least as well as the noisy rhetorical support for freedom of their conservative rivals.

Socialists of a social democratic persuasion can find good grounds for arguing that they led the way in making freedoms more meaningful for the majority of the population, while attempting, with some success, to combine their attachment to political liberty with a concern for social justice. As young and enthusiastic Communists, Mikhail Gorbachev and Zdeněk Mlynář discounted the crucial importance of institutionalizing political freedoms, but they were genuine seekers after social justice. Their lifetime's experience taught them that without democracy, some citizens would still be infinitely "more equal than others" and social justice under Communism would be thin gruel compared with what was on offer in the welfare states established in the social democratic countries of Northern and Western Europe.

While rejecting the view that almost everything could be left to the market, they nevertheless came to believe that market economies were more efficient than the Soviet-style command economy and that they were capable of producing significantly higher levels of social welfare. Gorbachev, born into a peasant family in southern Russia long after a Communist system had been established in the Soviet Union, and knowing no other socioeconomic order until well into his adulthood, came to see (as he puts it in the pages that follow) that "the system held everyone in its grip, stifling initiative. In order to protect itself, it suppressed both freedom of thought and any kind of searching or exploration." In addition to its dire political consequences, this held back economic development, except in certain selected areas where the nature of the centralized economy meant that disproportionately great resources could be directed. That applied, above all, to military industry and, for some years, to the space program.

In seeking to reform the Communist system, both of these politicians had to come to terms with unintended, as well as intended, consequences of their actions. Zdeněk Mlynář, the leading theoretician of the Prague Spring, had to face the fact that as a direct result of the attempted reform of the political and economic system in Czechoslo-

vakia his country became for a period of two decades still more politically oppressive than it had been in the years immediately preceding
the radical reforms of 1968. The Soviet armed intervention, which put
an end to the Prague Spring, not only led in 1977 to Mlynář's exile
from his homeland (after he had become an organizer and a signatory
of the oppositional Charter 77), but also had earlier brought to power
an unscrupulous political leadership far more responsive to Moscow
than to their own people.

For Mikhail Gorbachev the unintended consequences of introducing
transformative change of the Soviet polity were even more dramatic.
Along with his great achievements, not the least of which were leaving
his country *freer* than it had ever been and playing the key role in
ending the Cold War, were such unlooked-for results as the breakup
of the Soviet Union. The dismantling of the Soviet *system* was something that Gorbachev came to believe, in the course of his leadership
of the Communist Party, was both desirable and necessary. Had he not
used the powers of the General Secretaryship of the Soviet Communist
Party, to effect that—skillfully, peacefully, and by evolutionary
means—it is certain that Communism would not have ended when it
did and more than likely that it would still be the ideology in power
in Moscow. In contrast with change of the *system*, the breakup of the
Soviet *state* into fifteen pieces—the Soviet successor states—was entirely contrary to his intentions.

In historical perspective, though, it should be abundantly clear that
the positive results of Gorbachev's radical reforms greatly outweigh
the negative. Many observers, indeed, see the existence of fifteen states,
rather than one, on the territory of the former Soviet Union also as a
plus, though, of the successor states, only the Baltic countries of Es-
tonia, Latvia, and Lithuania are well on the way to establishing con-
solidated democracies. Russia, and one or two others, have hybrid
systems—a mixture of arbitrariness and democracy—and a majority
of these new members of the United Nations have unambiguously authoritarian regimes. For those who value democracy and the rule of
law above the ambiguous "right" of every nation (however defined) to
have its own state (a process opening up the prospect of almost infinite

regress), it remains far from clear that the complete breakup of the Soviet state should be welcomed. The independence of the Baltic states, whose forcible incorporation into the USSR in 1940 had never been accepted as legitimate either by the indigenous inhabitants or by the West, was a democratic necessity. It is highly doubtful, however, that the complete disintegration of the Soviet Union has furthered the cause of democracy as distinct from that of self-serving and corrupt national elites. Survey research in post-Soviet Russia shows conclusively that a majority of *Russians* came very quickly to regret the disintegration of the Soviet state, although most of them have been realistic enough to accept that it could not be put together again.[2]

By comparison with the momentous events that followed Gorbachev's coming to power in Moscow, the events of the Prague Spring may appear to pale almost into insignificance. Even in the Czech Republic today it is questionable whether the reformers of 1968 are given their due. It is worth noting that the reforms in Czechoslovakia and those in the Soviet Union were made by the same generation of Communists. However, there were some key differences in their political experience as well as some vital common influences. What is more, the reforms in Czechoslovakia and in the Soviet Union were initiated at different points in the life-cycle of party intellectuals in the two countries. The most important Soviet reformers in the perestroika years were "children of the Twentieth Party Congress." That is to say, they were people who had been young enough in 1956 to take to heart Khrushchev's denunciation of Stalinism at the Twentieth Congress of the Soviet Communist Party and to begin a process of reevaluating the system that had allowed Stalin to get away with such monstrous repression. By 1985 these anti-Stalinists, many of whom were to become anti-Leninists, were, for the most part, in their fifties and early sixties.

The key reformers in Czechoslovakia had also been profoundly affected by Khrushchev's "secret speech" of 1956, and the evolution of their political ideas, in the light of the Soviet leader's revelations, gathered speed faster than that of their Russian contemporaries. Since the Prague Spring preceded Gorbachev's perestroika by approximately twenty years, they were, accordingly, a younger group than their Soviet counterparts at the time when they attempted the radical reform of their system. The Czech (and some Slovak) reformers were people who had been particularly youthful and idealistic, eager to build a new world, in the early postwar years. Those in the same age cohort in the Soviet Union had been born into an established Communist regime that it was natural for them to take for granted. In contrast, Czechoslovakia between the wars had been a pluralist democracy before suffering from wartime Nazi occupation. In the immediate postwar years there was strong support for "socialism," variously defined, but within a pluralist framework. In actively supporting the Communist takeover of power in February 1948, many of Mlynář's generation did so for the best of motives, though their success produced the worst of outcomes. As a good Czech friend put it to me: "We were all twenty in 1948, so we were all forty in 1968." She also said: "We helped to get the country into this mess, so the least we could do was help get it out of it." The person who spoke these words was the late Rita Budínová (her maiden name which she retained when she was married to Zdeněk Mlynář).[3] Later, as Rita Klímová, she was the person who put the words "velvet revolution" into the English language when interpreting for her friend, Václav Havel. The speed of transformation in central Europe in 1989, made possible by the radical change of policy in Moscow, was such that at the beginning of that year Klímová was refused permission by the Communist authorities to go abroad for a holiday; before the end of it she had been appointed the first post-Communist Ambassador of Czechoslovakia to the United States.

The fact that the velvet revolution of 1989 occurred and was successful had almost everything to do with the change of course in Moscow. Very soon after becoming General Secretary Gorbachev had made it clear to the Communist leaders of Eastern Europe that there would be no more Soviet invasions to keep them in power if they could not retain the support of their own people. They may not have fully believed him then, but, to the dismay of a majority of them, they were to discover that he was serious. It was in 1988 that Gorbachev first made clear in public that the Soviet Union would not use military means to sustain unpopular political regimes, and the following year the peoples of Central and Eastern Europe took him at his word. The failure of the Prague Spring was due, not so much to the political limitations of the reformers within the Communist Party of Czechoslovakia and their non-party allies, but to the very different international political context twenty years earlier than the velvet revolution. The logic of developments—and the support for democracy of the majority of the people—was such that the substantial degree of pluralism that existed by the summer of 1968 would have developed into pluralist democracy within a relatively short space of time had there been no outside constraint in the shape of the Soviet Union (supported by hard-line leaders in most of the other East European Communist states). The most serious of the Czech reformers—among whom Mlynář was the principal author of the Action Program of the Communist Party in 1968, a document vehemently attacked both by Soviet and Czech Communist ideologues—always had to keep in mind the likely Soviet reactions to their proposals. Mlynář, knowing the Soviet Union better than many on the reformist wing of his party, was more sensitive than most of them to the likely extent of Soviet outrage. But reforms that were not radical enough for those in Czechoslovakia who ignored the international context turned out to be far too radical for the Soviet Politburo. The result was Soviet tanks on the streets of Prague and "normalization," Soviet-style, of political life in Czechoslovakia.

The United States, embroiled at the time in the Vietnam War, did not see what was happening in Czechoslovakia in the first eight months of 1968 as a particularly high foreign policy priority and, in any case, accepted the *de facto* division of the European continent whereby, whatever might be happening in this part of central Europe, it was firmly within the Soviet bloc. Thus, it makes little sense to blame the Prague Spring reformers for not being bolder when they produced greater freedom than the country had known for more than twenty years; when, if the movement had been allowed to run its course, it would inexorably have led to a more thoroughgoing democratization; and when, with all its limitations, it nevertheless was too much for the regional hegemon, the Soviet Union, to tolerate. It would be even more unjust to blame Mlynář and his associates for going as far as they did in reforming the Czechoslovak political system without permission of their Moscow overlords. To limit their reforms to what would be acceptable to the likes of Leonid Brezhnev and Mikhail Suslov would have been to exchange their remaining ideals for cynical careerism. At least they made the attempt to get their country out of the mess they had played a very minor role in getting it into, for when the Communists seized full power in 1948 a great many of the 1968 reformers had been late teenagers or twenty-year-old students.

As it happens, my own academic interest in the Prague Spring and my interest in reform of the Soviet political system—and its principal reformer, Mikhail Gorbachev—have a common link in the person of Zdeněk Mlynář, whom I first met in Prague in 1965. One day in Oxford in June 1979 I asked Mlynář if he knew anyone in the current Soviet leadership. "Only Gorbachev," he replied. Of course, Mlynář had *met* other Soviet leaders, including Leonid Brezhnev and Aleksei Kosygin, the General Secretary of the Communist Party and the Chairman of the Council of Ministers. But these meetings had been in the very special conditions of the tense relationship between Czech Communist reformers and an alarmed Soviet leadership during 1968. The most notable such occasion was when Mlynář joined Alexander Dubček and other leaders of the Czechoslovak Communist Party who had been forcibly brought to Moscow to take part in "negotiations" with a Soviet leadership that had just invaded their country. Under duress they attempted to achieve a compromise that would salvage something from the Prague Spring, heartened by the information that Mlynář was able to convey to his Czech colleagues—that within Czechoslovakia there was massive, albeit nonviolent, resistance by Czechs and Slovaks to the Soviet military intervention.

Zdeněk Mlynář, though, made it clear that his relationship with Gorbachev had been of a quite different nature to his close encounters of an unpleasant kind with the Soviet Politburo in 1968. They had known each other as students when they had studied together in the Law Faculty of Moscow University from 1950 to 1955 and had been in the same dormitory until Gorbachev's marriage to Raisa Titarenko in 1953.[4] Later I was to discover that Mikhail Gorbachev had, indeed, been Mlynář's closest Russian friend. And in an interview with a Russian journalist in July 1994, during which Gorbachev mentioned that he and Mlynář were taping the dialogue that is to be found in the pages that follow, he remarked that of all his friends, "[Zdeněk is] probably the person I'm closest to. He always has been."[5]

If Zdeněk Mlynář thought that my interest would be diminished by the fact that the one person in the Soviet leadership team he really knew was not yet a Politburo member but a Secretary of the Central Committee, appointed to that post less than a year previously to take responsibility within the party apparatus for agriculture, nothing could have been further from the truth. I told Mlynář that I was specially interested in Gorbachev because within the gerontocratic Soviet leadership he stood out for his comparative youth. Here was someone who had entered the top leadership team at the age of 47 and at the time of the 1979 conversation was only 48. Mlynář himself had become a member of the top Czechoslovak Communist Party leadership in 1968 at the age of 37 and was a member of its Presidium (Politburo) when just 38.

"Would you," I asked Mlynář, "say that Gorbachev has an open mind?" "Yes," he replied, "he's open-minded, intelligent, and anti-Stalinist." While there were a few members of the Soviet top leadership team at that time who possessed the second and still fewer who could claim, *sotto voce*, the third of these attributes, to the extent that Gorbachev possessed all three (in particular, a mind open to new experiences and new ideas) he was unique within the highest echelons of the party elite of the Brezhnev era—those whose faces adorned the front page of *Pravda* at the end of every Party Congress. Mlynář did not bring this assessment of his friend to the attention of a broader public until after Gorbachev had been chosen as General Secretary of the Central Committee of the Communist Party of the Soviet Union (CPSU) in March 1985. Then, he published a highly perceptive and informative article on "My Student Friend Mikhail Gorbachev" in the Italian Communist Party newspaper, *L'Unità*.[6] He was well aware that an endorsement from a Prague Spring "revisionist" who had been expelled from the Communist Party of Czechoslovakia in 1970 was an accolade Gorbachev could do without if he were to rise further within the CPSU hierarchy.

Mlynář, in his 1985 article—before his old friend had embarked on any of his reforms—observed that Gorbachev as a student had been unusual in taking Marxist theory seriously as distinct from a set of propositions that had to be learned by rote. He was someone who wished to understand the world around him rather than succumb either to ideological dogma or to unadulterated political pragmatism. He went on:

> Certainly Gorbachev today knows through experience what power is, what political practice is, and what distinguishes his world from that of theory. But I don't believe he is a man for whom politics and power have become ends in themselves. He has never been a cynic, and he is in character a reformer who considers politics as a means to an end, with its objective being to meet the needs of people.[7]

It was from Gorbachev that Mlynář learned about the gulf between the harsh realities of life in the Soviet countryside and the highly ideologized accounts of it they heard from some of their teachers in the Moscow University Law Faculty. Other teachers, however, opened their eyes to a wider intellectual universe. Their favorite professor was Stepan Fedorovich Kechekyan, who lectured on the history of political and legal thought. He had himself been educated before the 1917 revolution and was a scholar of genuine erudition.[8] For Gorbachev, in particular, given his peasant background and a schooling interrupted by war, the five years in Moscow University—notwithstanding the political climate of that era, which became noticeably less frosty after Stalin's death in March 1953—were, as he says in the pages that follow, a time when many things "began to change fundamentally" for him. "It was," he says, "a different world, a different atmosphere from the one I had lived in before then." Yet, as Gorbachev readily acknowledges, at that time "for me and others of my generation the question of changing the system in which we lived did not arise." He did not then connect the travails of his own family (both of his grandfathers were arrested at different times in the 1930s) and of his fellow-villagers with fundamental defects of the Soviet system or even with the culpability of Joseph Stalin. For Gorbachev and for Mlynář, as for so many Communists of their generation, Khrushchev's "secret speech" to the Twentieth Congress of the Communist Party of the Soviet Union was a turning-point. As Gorbachev says in his conversation with Mlynář: "I had no real idea of the true state of affairs up until the Khrushchev revelations, and even in 1985 when I became head of the party there was a lot I didn't know."

Endorsing the maxim that "A man's reach should exceed his grasp," the American political scientist Robert E. Lane has written: "Why? Because he will never know the extent of his grasp, his possibilities, unless he explores their outer limits. But if he extends his reach, he takes risks of disappointment."[9] Both Mlynář and Gorbachev extended their reach and suffered disappointment whether we measure political outcomes against their early misconceived ideals of a forced utopia or against their later aspirations to combine a socialist market economy with pluralist democracy. Moreover, both men finished up as social democrats, but neither the contemporary Czech Republic nor, still less, Russia is a social democracy. Yet both countries (especially the Czech Republic) are significantly closer to such a polity and society than they were in the days of either Brezhnev's Soviet Union or Husák's Czechoslovakia. Whatever social amelioration may have been practiced then, the two countries—and one system—suppressed personal freedom and political pluralism, in the absence of which there could be no social democracy.

Mlynář, in his conversations with Gorbachev, remarks: "Neither political successes nor political failures were ever the proof of the historical correctness of a policy. After all, even Nazism for many years seemed to be a political success in a certain sense. Therefore, I understand your [Gorbachev's] conviction that the criterion for the correctness of a policy is the kind of historical development it contributes to or, on the contrary, becomes a hindrance to." Communism was also, of course, a "political success in a certain sense"—and for much longer than fascism. There was a time when Western politicians actually feared that the Soviet Union was overtaking their countries economically, and for many of the poor—and a higher proportion of intellectuals—in Third World countries it was perceived as a model. The Soviet system survived, after all, for seven decades. Yet, in a book written in the early 1950s and published in 1955—a time when the strength of Soviet Communism was widely taken for granted—the British historian of the Russian Revolution and of the Soviet Communist Party, Leonard Schapiro, wrote:

> I do not share the predisposition of some contemporary historians, upon whom the hand of Hegel still lies somewhat heavily, in favour of the seemingly victorious side in history. Who are the victors, after all, and who the vanquished? . . . It would perhaps be wiser for the present to suspend the verdict as between Lenin and say Martov, or Plekhanov, or Chernov—or Struve, or even Stolypin.[10] The only really vanquished in history are, perhaps, those who cannot see anything beyond the apparent reality of immediate facts.[11]

Just as judgments of Communism as a success were premature, equally premature may be the consigning of perestroika as a failure or as a foolish attempt to "reform the unreformable." In the highly institutionalized, well-established Soviet system, the only place a serious reform—which, then, had the possibility of progressing beyond reform to transformative change—could realistically begin, if it were to stand a strong chance of success, was within the Communist Party. More generally in Communist systems it would have been exceedingly difficult for even an intra-party reform movement to prevail unless it had an active proponent in the person of the party leader, as was the case with Gorbachev, or at least a sympathetic listener as in the case of the First Secretary of the Communist Party of Czechoslovakia during the Prague Spring—the Slovak Alexander Dubček. Whereas a movement from below, Solidarity, played a large part in undermining Communism in Poland,[12] the way change came about in the second half of the 1960s in Czechoslovakia and the second half of the 1980s in the Soviet Union had much in common. In both cases reform initiatives originated within the ruling party, though liberalization then provided opportunities for the voices of non-Communist intellectuals (whether, for example, Václav Havel in Czechoslovakia or Andrei Sakharov in the Soviet Union) to be heard.

Czechoslovakia had an unusually high proportion of the population inside the Communist Party on the eve of the Prague Spring. Zdeněk Mlynář, in the conversations that follow, says: "In a political-organizational sense these parties comprised not only the ruling elite but also approximately 15 per cent of the population." The generalization has to be modified in the case of the Communist Party of the Soviet Union. It did, indeed, include the ruling elite (although many rank-and-file members could hardly be regarded as belonging to an elite) but shortly before Gorbachev came to power it embraced just 6.5 percent of the total population and about one in ten Soviet adults. In all the Communist countries membership was deliberately restricted to a minority of the population, so that the party could remain both strictly disciplined and internally coherent and thus able to exercise its "leading role" in society. If serious change took place within the party itself, that could not but have profound consequences for the country—and, in the Soviet case, for the whole of Eastern Europe. Yet the system was institutionalized to such a degree that even the General Secretary had to tread carefully if he wished to embark on reform. As Gorbachev observes in the pages that follow, "the slightest deviation from the established line was considered betrayal" and reform could not *begin* with "someone announcing that pluralism was necessary."

The evolution of the views of Mikhail Gorbachev and of Zdeněk Mlynář reached the point at which they ceased to think in terms of a "socialist market economy" or of socialism as a distinctive sociopolitical system, having little in common with what they would once have dismissed as "bourgeois democracy." An openness to democratic ideas from nonsocialist as well as social democratic sources came to characterize the outlook of both men, views they were freer to express in their enforced retirement from high office. Gorbachev expresses the standpoint clearly:

For myself I have renounced a deterministic scheme of things as put forward by the Soviet school of so-called Marxism. I see that it was wrong from the start to regard socialism as a special formation that represents something historically inevitable in the development of humankind. My whole experience has convinced me that a value-based conception of socialism is more correct. It is a process in which people seek to realize certain values, and in this process all progressive and democratic ideas and practical experiences are integrated.

One of the criticisms of Mikhail Gorbachev by his orthodox Communist colleagues, while he was still in power, was that he had stopped talking about a socialist system but, instead, increasingly spoke merely about "the socialist idea." He was criticized from a very different point in the political spectrum—that of the neoliberals—precisely for clinging to that "socialist idea." However, as was noted earlier in this introduction, the substance of Gorbachev's (as, indeed, of Mlynář's) understanding of socialism underwent fundamental change, and once freed of the constraints of being General Secretary of the Soviet Communist Party his understanding of "the socialist idea" became still more open-ended. As he puts it in the pages that follow: "The socialist idea is a search and an exploration. It may be only a contribution to a general process of exploration of various paths of development in the contemporary world. Genuinely historical ways of solving problems on the level of entire civilizations generally transcend the framework of ideologies; they lie on the other side of ideology."

Some may wonder why such a search should be described as in any way "socialist"; others may say, however such an approach is labeled, it amounts to no more than common sense. What needs to be underlined, however, is how far such thinking is removed from Marxist-Leninist ideology and, indeed, from ideological thinking in general. Gorbachev did not become *merely* a pragmatic politician. He continued to be interested in ideas and to cling to ideals. To a quite unusual degree, he learned from experience. It is not difficult to find contradictions between his statements at different times, especially during his

years in power when what he said frequently had to be adjusted to the
political exigencies of the time. He discovered that even in such a highly
authoritarian and centralized state as the post-Stalin Soviet Union (the
term used by Gorbachev and Mlynář is "totalitarian," which they apply not only to the Stalin period but to the post-Stalin Communist
system as well), there were constraints on the power of the top leader.
As Gorbachev says in this book, "a person at the heights of power
comes to see that he still can't achieve everything he thought possible."
Even on becoming General Secretary, he says: "I had to pay attention
to the overall circumstances, to the consequences of any steps I took,
and to the opinions of the other members of the leadership."

Thus, though the evolution of Gorbachev's ideas was tempered by
the realities of political power, the trajectory between the mid-1980s,
when he reached the highest office in the Soviet Union and the mid-
1990s when his recorded conversations with Zdeněk Mlynář came to
an end,[13] was in the direction of social democracy. Mlynář's own thinking had taken such a course earlier, given a massive stimulus by Soviet
armed intervention in his country and by his expulsion from the Communist Party which he had joined as a teenager. Some may detect a
stronger component of socialism, in a systemic, albeit non-Communist,
sense remaining in Mlynář's conception of social democracy than in
Gorbachev's. Yet both men came to view socialism in a way that seems
strikingly similar to that of the British philosopher Stuart Hampshire,
who wrote more than a quarter of a century ago:

> For me socialism is not so much a theory as a set of moral injunc-
> tions, which seem to me clearly right and rationally justifiable: first,
> that the elimination of poverty ought to be the first priority of gov-
> ernment after defence: secondly, that as great inequalities in wealth
> between different social groups lead to inequalities in power and in
> freedom of action, they are generally unjust and need to be redressed
> by governmental action; thirdly, that democratically elected govern-
> ments ought to ensure that primary and basic human needs are given
> priority within the economic system, even if this involves some loss

in the aggregate of goods and services which would otherwise be available.[14]

Hampshire was writing in a book devoted to "the socialist idea," which, along with comparison between the Prague Spring and perestroika, is a strong and recurring theme of the Gorbachev-Mlynář dialogue. Gorbachev and Mlynář, it would seem, reached by different routes the same view expressed by Hampshire in the penultimate sentence of the book he co-edited with Leszek Kolakowski, namely that "socialism needs a variety of evidence, open minds with moral conviction, and distrust of all unitary theories."[15]

The dialogue that follows benefits from the fact that the interlocutors were close friends. It would have been unthinkable for Zdeněk Mlynář to call Gorbachev by any name other than the diminutive, "Misha," and their political and personal affinity is such that he can press him on difficult points without causing offense. Mlynář is often the interrogator in these conversations and the level of trust and frankness between the two men is such that the answers he elicits sometimes go beyond anything Gorbachev has said hitherto in his own writings or in the countless interviews he has given to journalists. The conversations are a distillation of their experience—one that, in the first instance, clarifies for the two politicians themselves the nature of the journey they have undertaken. Their hope that it will also be found illuminating by others will surely be fulfilled. There is much still to be written about the rise and fall of Communism in the twentieth century. A younger generation, puzzled by the attraction that Communism once held for intellectuals and curious as to how it could be reformed and dismantled, will find that the Gorbachev-Mlynář conversations make an important contribution to understanding. They will encounter here the serious reflections of two former Communists who managed, notwithstanding the compromises that were an inextricable part of their political careers, to retain a moral sense and to continue to seek, but on surer foundations than the Marxism-Leninism of their youth, to build a better world.

ENDNOTES

1. Alec Nove, "New Thinking on the Economy," in Archie Brown (ed.), *New Thinking in Soviet Politics* (London: Macmillan, 1992), pp. 29–38, at 35–36.

2. On the basis of a careful study of survey data of the late Soviet and early post-Soviet era, Matthew Wyman has noted that only for an extremely brief period of time—at the end of 1991—did a majority of Russians extend their unwillingness to use force to hold the Soviet Union together to acquiescence with the breakup of the Union itself. See Wyman, *Public Opinion in Postcommunist Russia* (Basingstoke and London: Macmillan, 1997), pp. 172–73. More recently, Timothy J. Colton and Michael McFaul found, in a survey they conducted in 1999, that fewer than 15 percent of Russian citizens disagreed in whole or in part with the statement that the USSR "should never under any circumstances have been dissolved." Those who agreed with the statement outnumbered them by approximately five to one. See Colton and McFaul, *Are Russians Undemocratic?* (Working Paper of Carnegie Endowment for International Peace, No. 20, June 2001), p. 5.

3. Mlynář's widow is the sociologist, Irena Dubská-Mlynář, with whom he spent the last thirty years of his life, following the breakup of his marriage to Rita Budínová.

4. Zdeněk Mlynář was less than a year older than Mikhail Gorbachev. He was born on June 22, 1930. He died of cancer, at the age of 66, on April 15, 1997. Gorbachev was born on March 2, 1931, and more than seventy years later retains the energy and vigor of a younger man.

5. The interview was with Olga Kuchkina, columnist for the newspaper, *Komsomol'skaya Pravda*. It is reprinted in the Festschrift for Gorbachev published simultaneously in Russian and English in March 2001. See Valentin Tolstykh (ed.), *A Millennium Salute to Mikhail Gorbachev on His 70th Birthday* (Moscow: Valent, 2001), pp. 253–59; at pp. 255–56.

6. *L'Unità* (Rome), April 9, 1985, p. 9.

7. Ibid.

8. By coincidence, my academic supervisor when I first went to Russia on a British Council-sponsored exchange visit to Moscow University—for three months in early 1966—was none other than Professor Kechekyan, whom I, too, remember with respect and affection.

9. Robert E. Lane, *The Loss of Happiness in Market Democracies* (New Haven: Yale University Press, 2000), p. 314.

10. Yuliy Martov (1873–1923) broke with Lenin in 1903 and subsequently became leader of the Menshevik wing of the Russian revolutionary movement.

   Georgiy Plekhanov (1857–1918) was the first important Russian Marxist. His relations with Lenin varied over time, but in the last year of his life he headed a social democratic organization, Unity, which strongly opposed Lenin and the Bolsheviks.

Viktor Chernov (1873–1952) was leader of the Socialist Revolutionaries, a more moderate left-wing party than the Bolsheviks, and one that was definitively suppressed by Lenin in 1922.

Petr Struve (1870–1944) was a former social democrat who abandoned Marxism for liberalism and became a leading figure in that section of the pre-revolutionary liberal intelligentsia which stressed constitutionalism. Struve's break with Marxism was much influenced by the writings of the German social democrat Eduard Bernstein.

Petr Stolypin (1862–1911) was a Russian liberal conservative politician who made a big impact between 1906 and 1911. He held office as Minister of Interior and Chairman of the Council of Ministers and combined suppression of revolutionaries with the introduction of reform, especially in agriculture. He was assassinated in 1911. Anathametized throughout most of the Soviet period, he became a much respected politician, almost a cult figure, in post-Soviet Russia.

11. Leonard Schapiro, *The Origin of the Communist Autocracy: Political Opposition in the Soviet State. First Phase, 1917–1922* (London: The London School of Economics and Bell & Sons, 1955), p. x–xi.

12. Yet we do well to remember that Solidarity, after its spectacular success in mobilizing Polish workers in 1980–81, was forced into an underground existence following the imposition of martial law by the Polish party-state authorities in December 1981. It was not until 1989, as a consequence of the changes in Moscow, that Solidarity was able to reemerge victorious. How ephemeral political success can be was underlined in September 2001 when Solidarity won no seats in the Polish parliamentary elections and the most successful parties were the former Communists, the Democratic Left Alliance, and their partner, the small socialist Labor Union.

13. As noted earlier, Mlynář died in the Spring of 1997. Gorbachev came to Prague and spoke at his close friend's funeral. He also spent two hours speaking privately with Mlynář's widow. (Personal communications from Irina Dubská and from Mlynář's daughter, from his marriage to Rita Budínová , Milena Bartlová.)

14. Leszek Kolakowski and Stuart Hampshire (eds), *The Socialist Idea: A Reappraisal* (London: Weidenfeld and Nicolson, 1974), p. 249. Hampshire was Warden of Wadham College, Oxford, 1970–1984, having earlier held Chairs of Philosophy in London and Princeton and, subsequently (1985–91) at Stanford.

15. Ibid.

For the spelling of Russian names, I have generally used the more familiar and readable system of transliteration, without apostrophes to indicate the soft sign and usually with *y* rather than –i, -ii, –yi, –ij, or –yj. Thus we have Kechekyan (not Kechek'ian), Golyakov (not Goliakov), Trotsky (not Trotskii or Trockij), and Yeltsin (not El'tsin or Jel'cin).

Capitalization has been used for the terms Communist, Socialist, and Social Democratic when the reference is to particular organizations, political parties, movements, governments, and the like. When the emphasis is on general ideas, theories, principles, or the conception of a society based on those, capitalization is not used. The term "the party," unless otherwise specified, refers to the Communist Party or its equivalent, which was the only legal political party in countries that came to be dominated by Stalinism.

The authors use the term "civilization" in two special senses, notably in Conversation Three. One sense reflects a body of thinking among commentators on world politics since the end of the Cold War. The Cold War division between East and West, some argue, has been replaced by divisions among "civilizations," the main ones being Asian (China, Japan, etc.), Hindu (mainly India), Islamic, African, European, and American. But the authors also advocate a new *global civilization*, necessary to respond to and overcome potentially destructive global problems.

George Shriver
JANUARY 2002

Conversations with Gorbachev

This book, which Columbia University Press has kindly undertaken to present to American readers, is quite unusual in many respects. For one thing, in its original conception it was not oriented primarily toward an American audience. The book consists of edited transcripts of tape-recorded conversations between Zdeněk Mlynář, a prominent figure in Czech politics and public life, and myself.

Unfortunately, Dr. Mlynář, the coauthor of this book, died in April 1997. His name should be well known to those who followed the events surrounding the Prague Spring of 1968, a daring attempt by reformers in Czechoslovakia to liberalize and democratize the Communist system then existing in that country. Zdeněk Mlynář, along with Alexander Dubćek and other companions in struggle, did not simply take part in the Prague Spring. They were its initiators, its sources of inspiration, from the time when this democratization effort began until it was cut short by the military intervention of Warsaw Pact countries.

Fate brought Zdeněk and me together long before that. We were college classmates at the law school of Moscow University. We were at the same school, taking the same courses, attending the same lectures and seminars; but at our dormitory in the evenings we had stormy discussions of questions which at that time were troubling everyone, especially young people. Sometimes only the two of us were involved; at other times a wider group of students would join in. The mutual sympathy that took root then grew into a friendship that lasted almost half a century. We remained true to our friendship to the end, despite all the vicissitudes of our personal biographies and the trials and tribulations that befell our two countries. We were able to keep this friendship alive because we were bound, ever since our student days, by a closeness of views in our perception and understanding of the world. We were devoted to values held in common, and even during the most difficult and dramatic moments in relations between the USSR and Czechoslovakia we never regarded each other as standing on "opposite sides of the barricades."

In 1967, twelve years after graduating from Moscow University, Zdeněk and I met again as mature adults. I had invited him to visit me in my modest "homeland within a homeland," the Stavropol region, of which I was regional Communist Party secretary. Already behind us were the Twentieth Congress of the Soviet Communist Party [in 1956, at which Khrushchev gave his "secret speech" denouncing the crimes of Stalin], the suppression of the Hungarian uprising by Soviet troops [later in 1956], and further revelations of Stalin's crimes [for example, at the Twenty-Second Party Congress in 1961, followed by the 1964 removal of Khrushchev as party and government leader and a curbing of criticism of Stalin under Brezhnev].

We had a lot to discuss, and we shared our opinions and concerns with one another, as well as our hopes for the future. Zdeněk made no secret of the fact that he thought the political system in Czechoslovakia had to be democratized. On the whole we both concluded that our relations had not changed, that we remained true as ever to the hopes and dreams of our student days.

But circumstances conspired in such a way that twenty-two years passed before we could meet again. Those years were filled with historic events and processes that changed the fates of nations, and we were not only mere witnesses but active participants and even initiators of some of those events and processes. By the time we met again I was already General Secretary of the Central Committee of the Communist Party of the Soviet Union, leader of one of the major powers in the world. As for Zdeněk, he was a political exile. Because he had been one of the leaders of the Prague Spring and, later, was one of the authors and signers of the famous protest document, Charter 77, the authorities then in power in Czechoslovakia had pressured him into leaving his homeland, and he had established himself in Vienna.

It may seem surprising, but even in those circumstances, which were totally new, both for our countries and for ourselves personally, we still understood each other perfectly, just as if those twenty-two years had not intervened. It turned out that our separate appraisals of what had occurred during those years in our two countries and in the world as a whole coincided. Our political views, despite all the differences in the personal experiences we had gone through, were basically in agreement.

From then on we maintained fairly regular contact, keeping in touch by mail and by phone. Finally, after I was obliged to leave my post as president of the USSR, an idea ripened in our minds—namely, to have a more detailed joint discussion about what we had lived through during the preceding decades, our hopes and disappointments, our new discoveries and false starts, to try to reflect more deeply on the dramatic twists and turns in the fates of our countries and the whole world.

We could take advantage of a special privilege—by that time we could think out loud about everything without limitations, without taking care to speak in conventional, official terms. Our tape-recorded conversations took place, in several separate sessions, from November 1993 to June 1994. We wanted first of all to sort out our own thoughts and feelings in regard to our past political activities, to help one another understand better why each of us had done what he had done, what we had succeeded in accomplishing and what we had not, and to what extent we had acted correctly at one or another moment. To the extent that we had arrived at similar views by separate paths, it was important to us, for that reason, to try to explain to one another those areas where our views did not completely coincide. This involved events in which we had been witnesses and participants, as well as problems for which we were both seeking solutions. Therefore, in these most friendly conversations, some polemicizing occurs occasionally, but these are polemics between friends seeking to understand one another and searching for what is called "the Truth."

Since it occurred to us from the very beginning that our conversations might be of interest to the broader public, we tape-recorded them. That is how this book came into being. We had no intention of reproducing in this book all our many hours of conversation. Instead we selected those passages which, it seemed to us, would be of the greatest interest to the widest circles, including those beyond the borders of the Czech Republic and Russia.

In paying tribute to the memory of my friend Zdeněk, I consider it my duty to emphasize the special contribution he made to this book. As the reader will see, he was the "lead horse" on our team: the one who most often raised new questions, initiated topics for discussion, including the most difficult for both of us, concerning our personal responsibility for the actions and measures we took, whose consequences sometimes weighed heavily on the fates of many other people. These questions also included our own illusions or miscalculations, missed opportunities, and possible alternatives that we did not pursue.

Zdeněk shared his doubts and questions, such as the following: Should he [and his associates] really have begun something that could end in defeat? Shouldn't they have acted more cautiously? Was it really worth trying, in general, to reform (and thereby save) something that was sooner or later doomed to collapse?

This, of course, was an expression of the restless, searching nature of this remarkable individual, his innate and acute sense of conscience, his skeptical bent of mind, his striving in all things to dig down to the essence, the heart of the matter, his willingness to engage in discussion without any equivocation. In Zdeněk there arose early in life an inclination toward theoretical reflection on social problems, and after his forced retirement (when he was only 38 years old), followed by his time in exile in Vienna, he concentrated entirely on theoretical work and writing about public affairs, as well as thinking over the lessons of the Prague Spring, and in this respect he accomplished an enormous labor, publishing several books and many articles. The results of his probing research into contemporary problems are reflected in the pages of this book. Zdeněk was then at the height of his intellectual powers. After our book was published in the Czech language in 1995 he wanted it to come out in Russian as soon as possible. A Russian edition is still awaited. Zdeněk would of course have been overjoyed to know that our book was also published in the United States.

This book is about things that happened to all of us during the past five or six decades, not just to those who lived in the so-called socialist camp but to everyone who was directly or indirectly affected by the dramatic conflicts of the second half of the twentieth century—the Cold War confrontation between two nuclear superpowers, which brought the world to the brink of disaster; the insane arms race; local wars and severe international crises; the difficult search for a way out of the Cold War impasse; the democratic revolutions in the Soviet bloc countries; the reunification of Germany; the dissolution of the USSR; and many other events about which arguments continue all over the world to this day.

Two processes, which had determined my fate and his—the Prague Spring in Czechoslovakia and perestroika in the Soviet Union—served of course as the axis of our discussions, but into this orbit many other questions were drawn.

Tormentedly, for many years, Zdeněk had reflected on the lessons of the Prague Spring. That had been his "finest hour," when his star was in its ascendancy, and he remained true always to the principles that had inspired the Prague reformers of 1968. But he also had an intense feeling of personal responsibility for the consequences of the Prague Spring, including the consequences of military intervention. It is no accident that he posed the first question, at the very beginning of our conversations, as follows: "Why exactly did we join the Communist Party?" (Incidentally, he joined the Communist Party of Czechoslovakia at the age of 16, whereas I became a candidate member of the Communist Party of the Soviet Union at the age of 19 and joined the party as a second-year university student at the age of 21.) The point at issue, of course, was our attitude toward Communism as an ideology and as a system. Readers can see for themselves how we answered that question. Still, membership in the Communist Party is how our commonly shared political biography began, one that led him subsequently to become a leader of the Prague Spring in Czechoslovakia and me to become a leader of perestroika in the Soviet Union.

I perceived the events of the Prague Spring in 1968 as a possibility for renewal, for an unleashing of the creative potential in the socialist system—that was my understanding of things then. I wished success to this process of reform. But things ended up with the introduction of Warsaw Pact troops into Czechoslovakia, primarily Soviet troops, in fact. For Zdeněk this was an expression of political reaction, of Stalinist restoration, a blow against the reform-minded forces in the Communist Party of Czechoslovakia who were seeking a democratic renewal of socialism. For me, it was a dramatic and painful event, but one I thought necessary for the defense of socialism against subversive activities on the part of the Western powers. That was the kind of thinking that prevailed among the majority of my fellow citizens, not without the influence of the mass propaganda that was unleashed in our country, although some people did go out and protest in Moscow, on Red Square, and in other Soviet cities.

A year later I chanced to visit Czechoslovakia as part of an official Soviet delegation. We went to Prague, Bratislava, Brno, and a number of other cities, as well as to rural areas. This visit overturned all my conceptions. I saw that the people of Czechoslovakia had not welcomed our intervention, that we had humiliated them; in the eyes of the Czechs and Slovaks we had become occupation forces. At the factories that we visited workers turned away from us. This was a shock to me. From that time on I began to think more and more about what was going on in our country, and I came to an unconsoling conclusion: there was something wrong in our country. An understanding ripened in my mind: the actions of the Brezhnev leadership had been dictated not only by the threat that the "socialist commonwealth" might fall apart but also by the internal situation in the Soviet Union. The time was ripe for change in our own country, and they were using this as a way of putting off such changes.

The difficult and painful experiences that befell Zdeněk did not break his spirit. He continued to be active in defense of the choice he had made, a choice made also by millions of Czechs and Slovaks. The beginning of perestroika in the Soviet Union restored his hopes for change in the Soviet system. As he himself acknowledges, the election of Gorbachev as general secretary had an intense impact on him personally: previously, in his view, a "Moscow Spring" had seemed hardly possible. But knowing me, he assumed I would pursue a policy of reform. Still, how far would Gorbachev be able to go? Great doubts had arisen in Zdeněk's mind in regard to the prospects for democratic change in Soviet society. At the same time he caught himself thinking: "Is my own defeat in 1968 the reason for my pessimism? Is that interfering with my ability to assess things more objectively?"

I must give credit where credit is due. Despite all his doubts, my friend Zdeněk immediately and publicly, in the press and on television and in meetings with Western politicians and public figures, took a clear stand in support of Gorbachev and the policies of perestroika. He had every right to say (and the reader will find this in our book): "At that moment I was the only person in the West who knew you personally." He knew me and trusted me. People came to him for consultation, not just journalists but also politicians, diplomats, and, as he puts it, "specialists in information gathering," and he told them that he could say with an easy conscience: "Gorbachev will carry out fundamental changes in both domestic and foreign policy."

During my years as leader of the Soviet Union fundamental democratic changes were indeed carried out, and I found support for this not only in my country but also among many friends abroad. One of them was Zdeněk, my unforgettable friend, whose support and solidarity I especially treasured.

I hope that American readers will take an understanding attitude toward the special kind of political terminology we use in our conversations. I have in mind especially the term "socialism," which readers will frequently encounter in these pages. This term has its origins in the time of the Enlightenment in Europe, but many misconceptions are now connected with it. The word has often been misused and its meaning distorted beyond recognition.

Our formative years, Zdeněk's and mine, were in a society which called itself socialist and which was called that by others, including many people in the West. But it actually was not socialist, because true socialism is unthinkable without democracy. Many people in the West equate socialism with "Communism," and both are associated in their minds with repressive regimes of the Stalinist type.

It took a certain amount of time for Zdeněk Mlynář and myself, gradually, on the basis of our own experience and acquaintance with other trends of social thought and other viewpoints, to overcome the dogmatic conception of socialism that had been drilled into us (in the context of a closed society) from the time we sat at our desks as students. This dogma conceived socialism as a separate, special social formation called upon to replace capitalism as the result of certain general laws of history. As readers will see and, I hope, be persuaded, the understanding of socialism that we arrived at differs in principle from the schematic determinism that many Marxists were enthralled by for so long, not to mention the ideological dogmas of Soviet Marxism.

In discussing the fate of the socialist idea in the past, present, and future, Zdeněk and I proceeded from a *value-based* vision of socialism, one to which Western European Social Democracy adheres, as many people know. In my estimation, freedom, equality, justice, and solidarity—and, importantly, the interconnectedness of these values—rank highest of all among socialist values. Today I am engaged in an effort to establish in Russia a new, mass-based Social Democratic Party. Therefore for me these values also signify the freedom to choose a particular socio-political orientation or program, one that includes such notions as access for all to education and adequate health care, a socially oriented market, and a definite minimum guarantee of social support to disadvantaged sections of the population. Of course, all this requires that government play a role. This is indispensable because the market by itself does not and cannot provide for these things to the full extent necessary.

From this point of view, I consider the traditional contrast drawn between socialism and liberalism to be outdated, a tradition that has exhausted itself. During the twentieth century, the liberals were obliged to borrow something from the socialists (the principle of social justice, for example, and of government regulation of the economy), while the socialists borrowed from the liberals (the ideas of political pluralism and competition on the open market). The resulting synthesis is a fruitful one—one capable, I am convinced, of playing a positive role in the search for answers to the global challenges of the present time. I am sure that these answers must be sought beyond the bounds of the supposed dichotomy between socialism and capitalism. For a long time now that "dichotomy" has not corresponded to the complex reality of the interconnected and interdependent modern world.

In these conversations it was important for us to define anew our attitude toward the idea of socialism in light of the transformations our societies and the world around us have undergone in the last several decades. We have stated that we remain socialists, but we do not block ourselves off from other trends of democratic and humanist thought. Any wearing of ideological blinders in relation to that which is different or "other than ours"—any manifestation of fundamentalism—is counterproductive and dangerous.

There is one other aspect that I cannot fail to emphasize.

Today, after thinking over the experience of perestroika, and all of Soviet history, after reflecting on present-day realities, the difficulties and dangers, and possible variant paths of development for our world as it undergoes globalization, I have arrived at the conviction that if it is worth talking about socialism at all in our times, then it must be done as a politically active person.

For me, on the whole, this conclusion is simply a matter of logic. When I began perestroika it was precisely politics that I had to keep in mind. This of course meant changing the politics of the CPSU, which had led our country into a blind alley and which was pushing the world in the direction of a nuclear confrontation. Incidentally, to this very day dogmatists on the left and on the right rebuke me for not presenting my programmatic aims in full, for not announcing a schema that I would follow. My view was and is that a fanatical belief in wonder-working schemas, irrefutable dogmas, plans, and programs, which have never been carried out, beginning from 1917, would undermine the possibility of our great country having a real and normal process of development.

Of course politics will vary from country to country, even if "native" parties function as members of international organizations (Socialist International, "Liberal International," "Conservative International," etc.). Such parties will invariably carry out policies guided by national interests, while taking the international context into account (whether effectively or not is another question). But every form of politics has a more or less different world view in the background. And such world views vary from one another, although in our times this is less and less true, even if we are talking about parties as different as, let us say, Social Democrats and neoconservatives.

Thus in "socialism" as I now understand it there is a subtext, a world view in the background, consisting of the values I have listed above. Meanwhile, politics, in spite of everything, is a practical and pragmatic matter. It is changeable, depending on circumstances and even the temporary conjuncture of circumstances. And domestic politics will merge more and more with international politics in the coming globalized world.

Today, when the opposition between democracy and Communist totalitarianism is a thing of the past, the significance of a politics that will correspond to the realities of our new world becomes especially vital. The problems with which politics has to deal are increasingly severe. This is true of the industrially developed countries, the relations between developed and developing countries, and the world as a whole. I hope that from this point of view as well, in the way we address these problems, American readers will find our book rewarding.

Mikhail Gorbachev
MARCH 2002

The Criss-Crossing of our Paths

1. STUDENT COMMUNISTS

Why We Joined the Communist Party

Z.M.   It would be worthwhile to begin our conversation with the question of why exactly we joined the Communist Party. The answer for each of us will probably be distinctly different, but at the same time this is where our common political biography begins. So I'll start right off by trying to answer that question for myself.

In general and on the whole this was not even connected, properly speaking, with my concepts of socialism. The decisive consideration was the war [World War II]. When the war ended I was fifteen years old, and not especially interested in social problems, even less in politics. While I was a high school student [at a secondary school that provided a classical education and prepared students for college], I wanted to go on to study zoology. But this was during the German occupation, and I lived in a kind of constant state of unconscious fear. As a Czech I knew that the Nazis considered the Czech people an inferior race, and if Hitler emerged victorious, my fate might be the same as that of my Jewish classmates. It is mainly for that reason, it seems, that the end of the war had a very powerful effect on me. Somehow there suddenly arose within me, almost automatically, of its own accord, a sense that the world had changed, that an entirely different era had begun, and that now a person could not stand aside from the course of events.

The main victor in the war in my eyes had been Stalin; those in power in the Soviet Union were the Communists. Everyone knew that a different system existed there, a *socialist system.* At that time I automatically considered this system better, more just, and stronger than the one under which I had lived up to that point. I had a rather vague notion, but one I couldn't get rid of, that most likely this was the prototype of the future.

In a word, if I wanted to answer this question now briefly, using contemporary political terminology, I would say that in 1946 at the age of sixteen I joined the Communist Party in the hope that that party would change social relations and the social situation in such a way that they would become more just, that there would be no more war, and that Nazism would never again be a threat to other nations, that it would be eliminated for good.

M.G.   I will answer this question spontaneously, thinking out loud, as it were, the way one does when talking with a friend. For me there were probably two aspects that were of fundamental importance. First, there was the example of my grandfather (on my mother's side) and of my father. My grandfather had been a poor peasant, and beginning from a very early age, after the death of his father, he had to be concerned about a family in which there were five children. During World War I my grandfather was on the Turkish front, and he returned from the war with a definitely radical outlook, which was typical of the soldiers at that time. Then after the revolution, when the family was given the land it worked on, my grandfather was won over completely to the side of the Soviet government. In the oral history of our family it was constantly repeated: the revolution gave our family land. For that reason I viewed my grandfather's joining the party in 1928 as a perfectly logical step, along with his direct participation in the reorganization of village life on a new basis.

Then came 1937. My grandfather was arrested as an "enemy of the people." He was held for fourteen months of investigation, in the course of which he underwent cruel torture. I suddenly found myself a member of a family of an enemy of the people. And so at that time the drama of 1937–38 was part of my own direct experience. For our conversation what is important is the fact that when my grandfather returned from prison and told about everything that had happened there, neither then nor at any other time did he say anything bad about the Soviet government. In his view, Stalin had not known about these crimes. Moreover, as he saw it, those who had carried out these crimes had themselves been made to pay: some were arrested; some even shot themselves. And so it would seem, the later wave of repression over- took—and justifiably—those who were to blame for the sufferings of the people. A certain crafty and perfidious tactic on Stalin's part was evident here.

My father, who married the daughter of a Communist, was com- pletely on his side, even though his own father, my other grandfather, refused for a long time to join the collective farm, remaining an indi- vidual farmer instead.

z.m. Thus in your family, so to speak, both of the historical tenden- cies of development in the Russian countryside were represented.

m.g. Yes, you could put it that way. And an important thing for me was that my father became a Communist, joining the party while he was at the front during the war. You are absolutely right that for us the war was not only a great victory over fascism but proof that our country's cause was the right one. And by the same token, so was the cause of Communism.

That was how we viewed things. To that I should add that there was something in my very nature, in my personality. (I can talk about this now, sort of looking at myself from the outside.) From my earliest days I liked to be a leader among my peers—that was my nature. And this remained true when I joined the Komsomol, the Young Commu- nist League, and later when I joined the party—it was a way of some- how realizing my potential. I became a candidate for party membership as early as 1950, when I was still in high school, and two years later I was accepted as a member of the Communist Party of the Soviet Union (CPSU) while a student at Moscow University.

So the main thing for both of us was our ideological motivation, not pragmatic considerations of some other kind.

Communist True Believers

Z.M.   I consider all this important for an understanding of the motivation behind our decisions to join the party. People for whom Communism no longer offered any hope, who knew that joining the Communist Party was for most of them a necessary condition for a further successful career, that a party membership card was often a kind of "pass" that opened the door to a comfortable existence—such people transpose all that kind of thinking back into the era of our youth, that is, fifty years ago. They suspect that in all likelihood we based ourselves even then on considerations of careerism and timeserving.

It would be worthwhile now for us to talk about how we pictured socialism and communism. Because after joining the party we did not remain members only on the basis of the reasons that brought us there. We were there in order to help "change the world" based on certain conceptions corresponding to Communist ideology. When I went to Moscow in 1950 to study at the university and we first met, I was no longer exactly the apolitical youngster that I had been in 1946. I considered myself a conscious Communist. By that time I had already read not only various party pamphlets but also Stalin's *History of the All-Union Communist Party (Bolshevik)* with its famous chapter on dialectical and historical materialism. I had read Stalin's *Problems of Leninism,* Lenin's *State and Revolution,* Engels's *Anti-Duehring,* and of course *The Communist Manifesto.* By then I thought I knew the "fundamentals of Marxism," but of course it was not so much knowledge of Marxism as the case of a self-confident person who didn't really know anything but who unceasingly told himself that by having read these books he had come to understand the laws of development of the human race and the world as a whole. As I have said several times since then, I was not knowledgeable but I was "politically aware." I hardly knew anything really, but I could pass judgment on everything and everyone as to whether they were progressive or reactionary.

Communist ideology became for me like a faith or religion, and I acquired all the traits typical, for the most part, of fanatical believers. This means first of all intolerance toward nonbelievers. Also, that any

oppression and persecution of them is justified. My concept of socialism was quite simple: for me it meant a social system in which undesirable capitalist relations, that is, private property and the exploitation
associated with it, had been eliminated; a system in which there was
social justice and, most important, where everything was administered
rationally and scientifically. And because such a system supposedly already existed in practice in the USSR, I made every effort to gain the
possibility of studying in Moscow itself. You, on the other hand, were
born there and grew up there, so that your approach to Communist
ideology and the concept of socialism must have been different then.

M.G. Not only I, but the generation before me, took as an existing
reality, as a given, everything that had taken place under Communist
rule; we took it as a given that the system we lived under was socialism.
That's how I understood things even before I read any Marxist literature. But at this point I must comment on the school system: it played
an enormous role in forming our ideas about the world; it sought to
convince us by all means at its disposal that we were living in the most
just form of society. Thus we developed the outlook, in reference to
the reality in which we were living, that no alternative was possible.

But even in the last years of high school, we talked about many
things in a very critical way, based of course on our own experience
and only on the local level; above all we were critical of the way of life
of the representatives of local government. In embryonic form, this was
a critique of the *nomenklatura* [the upper ranks of Communist Party
and government officials in the hierarchical Stalinist system—Trans.].
But socialism for us, as I've said, was something for which there was
no alternative.

Z.M. On the other hand, the possibility of an alternative did exist for
me. After all, most of my peers had not accepted Communist ideology.
I saw in Communism a better alternative than prewar Czechoslovakia.
Although I had been just a boy before the war, I was aware not only
of the weakness of the government which had capitulated to Hitler but
also that the Western Allies—England and France—had betrayed us

and sold us out to Hitler at Munich. I had also observed social injustice and poverty. Our family had not been directly affected—my father had been an officer. But we lived at army bases in Slovakia, and both poverty and deprivation were present everywhere there at the time. So I preferred socialism as an alternative, a system that was better, more just, more rational, and stronger.

M.G.   Communist ideology was very attractive for young people then. That is true. The front-line soldiers came back from the war, most of them young people, filled with the pride of victory. And they had seen another world, the world of Europe, even though what they had seen had suffered from the destruction of the war. They were convinced that after the war's end, life in our country too would begin to change— not only that the horrors of war would not be repeated but that the suffering of the 1930s would also be a thing of the past. Nevertheless, their concept of the future never went beyond the framework of Communist ideology, which sang the praises of social justice and people's power.

The knowledge acquired in school, above all from history, confirmed that neither the tsarist system in Russia nor the colonial system of the European powers, neither crises nor wars—none of those things were merely inventions of propaganda. That is why for me and for others of my generation the question of changing the system in which we lived did not arise.

Z.M.   It could be said that our original conception of socialism simply equated socialism with the kind of system that existed in the USSR. Or when we thought about this on a world scale, socialism began in those countries where a Communist Party had come to power. We saw things in this way for various reasons, but in the end we saw it in quite a similar way. That did not mean that we rejected any criticism of existing conditions. On the contrary, we considered it necessary in the name of Communist ideals to criticize and change the existing reality, which both of us tried to do in subsequent years on the practical level. And then we came to a reappraisal of our views. But before all that happened we both had been supporters and proponents of Communist ideology in the form in which it had existed in Stalin's time. Here, as the saying goes, you can't drop any words from the song. And that left its mark on the process of our formation as individuals.

How We Viewed the Stalin Terror

Z.M.   For myself I must say that even during the war I had of course heard about, and later I even read about, the political trials in the USSR. But for a long time I thought Stalin's terror was a matter of history, something like the terror that also accompanied the French revolution. At the same time I had no idea of the scale of the political terror in Stalin's time, no notion of the fact that innocent people had confessed to crimes when they could no long endure torture. Any talk about such things I simply considered to be anti-Communist propaganda.

However, this quickly stopped being just a theoretical question for me, because after 1948 the Stalin terror gradually began in Czechoslovakia, as elsewhere. In truth I must say that for a long time I agreed with the idea of suppressing the opponents of Communism and enforcing various kinds of discrimination against them: after all, they were opposed to historical progress, so why give them a chance to spread various kinds of reactionary heresy?

I also approved of the idea that such people should not be allowed, let's say, to study at the university level or hold responsible posts, and so forth. I did not protest against the political trials. Inwardly I sought to convince myself that this was necessary, that it was a natural manifestation of the revolutionary process, as had occurred before in history. But I could not admit to myself even the idea that the charges and the political trials of that time might simply be fabrications, that the confessions might have been extorted by torture. When, in 1952, top party leaders were brought to trial, headed by the general secretary of the Communist Party of Czechoslovakia (CPC), Rudolf Slánský, it occurred to me that both the charges in the indictment and the confessions of the accused were too much like exaggerated propaganda.

But I could not have imagined that all of this had been fabricated, that both the accused and the accusers had been obliged to learn by heart an entire trial scenario that had been written out in advance. All this I learned only in 1956, and for me it was a great shock. When the trial was going on I had seen in some of the charges that were given big play at the time an explanation of why after 1948 fear of dictatorial methods in the party had begun to circulate even among Communists. It was similar to the way your grandfather thought that those who had jailed him were wreckers and deserved their fate when they were later denounced and arrested.

M.G.   I had no real idea of the true state of affairs up until the Khrushchev revelations, and even in 1985 when I became head of the party there was still a lot I didn't know.

Z.M.   In my case such a concept [that the trials were fabricated] never occurred to me, partly because of the way I myself looked at these things. I don't know if you remember the time at a seminar on criminal law I defended the argument that in political trials the presumption of innocence did not apply. That was precisely during the Slansky trial in Prague, and I sincerely asserted that, after all, the decision about the guilt of the accused had been handed down by the political leadership and the court had simply drawn the legal conclusions. The seminar was being conducted by a graduate student whose name I don't remember, but he was very much frightened by all this . . .

M.G.   Poor fellow!

Z.M.   . . . And he avoided answering, referring me instead to the seminar on Marxism-Leninism. So since I thought and reasoned in that way, I could not know about the Stalin terror. I could not know even as much as under a different state of affairs I could have known, what I could have arrived at by thinking things out on my own. Although all this was a result of a deformed way of thinking, nevertheless, a certain kind of honesty did remain: that is, I openly said what I was thinking and refused to hypocritically assert that the presumption of innocence was being observed when in fact it was not.

M.G.   All this is one of the most painful pages in our past. Before Khrushchev and the Twentieth Congress of the CPSU, this was something that nobody talked about in general. And after Khrushchev they began to try to suppress what had started under him, what could be designated as the beginning of a break with Stalinism. Only after Khrushchev's speech at the Twentieth Congress did I begin to understand the inner connection between what had happened in our country and what had happened to my family. My memories and associations from childhood became interwoven with the beginnings of an awareness of what Stalinism was.

People had trouble accepting all this. After graduating from the university I went to Stavropol, and in 1956 I was one of those from the Komsomol who on party instructions traveled from place to place to explain the significance of Khrushchev's speech on the Stalin personality cult. Among party officials the reaction was very guarded; many of them simply had a negative reaction. In their view the repression of the 1930s was justified by the fact that, as they put it, people were arrested who earlier had forced the peasants to join the collective farms. For my own part I accepted Khrushchev's speech. Yet Stalin's death, for you and me, and not only for us, had been a heavy blow that we found hard to endure. All night long we were part of the crowd going to see his coffin.

Z.M.   Yes, I remember us standing side by side in the auditorium on Hertzen Street during the two minutes of silence [to acknowledge Stalin's death], and I remember asking you: "Misha, what's going to happen to us now?" And you in a voice full of alarm and uneasiness, answered, "I don't know." Our world, the world of true-believing Stalinist Communists, was beginning to fall apart.

Knowledge Undermines Belief

M.G.   Yes, that's the way it was. But for my own part I must say that, in spite of everything, when I came to Moscow University a lot of things began to change fundamentally for me. It was a different world, a different atmosphere from the one I had lived in before. Unlike most Soviet institutions of higher learning of those days, in which one spent one's time mainly at rote learning, Moscow University provided quite a few opportunities for discussion and debate and freedom of thought, although perhaps I overdid it somewhat, giving in to the mood of the place. Nevertheless, probably the most important things we gained there came as a result of contact with outstanding university professors.

z.M.   Yes, especially with professors of the old school . . .

M.G.   . . . like Kechekyan, who lectured on the history of political thought. He opened up an entire world of ideas for us: the Vedas of India, Confucianism, Plato and Aristotle, Machiavelli and Rousseau. The history of human thought, a world we had not known, excited our minds. And we studied all these things as devoted servants of the state; that is, we connected what we studied with the problems of the structure of our society and politics. Last of all, it was the university that opened my eyes to the truth of Marxism itself. I was especially attracted by the polemical writings of the Marxists, which allowed me to become familiar with their arguments—not only theirs, however, but also the arguments of their opponents.

z.M.   Although we cannot fail to speak about one-sidedness. We knew about Kautsky, of course, that he was a renegade, but we did not read any of his writings. But what you say is true. Besides that, I remember an incident after a lecture on the history of the CPSU in which Professor Golyakov discussed the fact that Lenin after the revolution had given Martov, the main leader of the Mensheviks, the opportunity to emigrate to the West. I remember after that you said to me: "Look, Lenin didn't even go so far as to arrest Martov." This was said when Stalin was still alive. I understood that as an expression of your negative attitude toward the trials Stalin had staged.

I also referred to this incident in an article published in the West after you had become the head of the CPSU in 1985. A certain learned "Sovietologist," whose name I no longer remember, wrote in reply to my article that I had made all this up, that it was a projection backwards from the Khrushchev era, that there weren't any students who could have known anything like that under Stalin. But the fact is that Professor Golyakov, who had been an Old Bolshevik and who had worked for many years as chairman of the Supreme Court of the RSFSR, actually did tell us about the Lenin-Martov incident way back then, and I personally remember it very well.

M.G.   Yes, we had good luck with our university. We lived under unique conditions for that time, conditions characterized by a certain degree of freedom and a creative atmosphere. We were provided with high-quality knowledge and we learned how to think. And all that was a great help to us in our future life. Before the university I was trapped in my belief system in the sense that I accepted a great deal as given, as assumptions not to be questioned. At the university I began to think and reflect and to look at things differently. But of course that was only the beginning of a prolonged process.

Z.M.   Yes, I think that we began to take a different attitude, in part, even toward Communist ideology at the university. I remember a seminar on Lenin's book *State and Revolution*. This was already after Stalin's death. I gave a report at that seminar on the so-called economic-organizing functions of the state. And although I tried very hard, I could not find in Lenin's writings the propositions Stalin put forward about the role of the state and of law in the economy. Those propositions, after all, lay at the basis of the entire system of centralized, administrative-command type of economic planning. Aside from the notion that under socialism everyone would be working for "one single factory," which in fact could be a justification for totalitarianism—

which of course didn't occur to me at the time—Lenin actually said
only that the state would have to provide for the distribution of goods
according to the principle "to each according to their work." I went
into all this in detail in my report, and as a result I came up, indirectly,
with a theoretical critique of the then-official understanding of the
"economic-organizational functions of the state."

I remember that you agreed with me as far back as when I was
preparing that report and later when it was discussed at the seminar.
Much later, somewhere around 1986 or 1987, I discovered in one of
your speeches the same kind of formulation of these ideas. For me these
ideas played no small part in 1967 when we were drafting proposals
on how to overcome the Stalinist model of public administration. But
the original seed of these thoughts sprouted back then at the university
seminar in Moscow in 1953 or 1954.

Early Shoots of Independent Thought and a Sense of Responsibility

Z.M.   We took our leave of the university in the summer of 1955, so
that the decisive political turning point represented by Khrushchev's
criticism of Stalin took place after we were no longer students. But I
think that precisely because of those five years of study at Moscow
University, Khrushchev's speech was somewhat less shattering for me
then for my friends and comrades in the Communist Party in Czechoslovakia. What I have in mind is not so much the revelations about the
large-scale and brutal methods of political terror and the revelations
about the politically inspired trials under Stalin. That was unexpected
for me, as I've already said, and I simply could not have imagined it.
But on the other hand, a general change of political line could be sensed
in Moscow after 1953, and evidently it could be sensed more strongly
there than in Prague, where only three months before Stalin's death,
eleven persons were executed as a result of the Slansky trial.

Something of great significance for my understanding of socialism
happened as early as the spring of 1955 when Khrushchev flew to
Belgrade, where he called Tito a "good comrade" and with great ceremony proclaimed, together with Tito, the principle that different

roads to socialism are possible. For you in the USSR these were questions of foreign policy, but for us in the so-called people's democracies (the term that was used in those days) this was something altogether different. It was at that very time that the party leadership was issuing the harshest reprimands if any us seemed to deviate from the so-called Soviet model. Moreover, the party functionaries who had been executed as a result of the rigged show trials were accused, on top of everything else, of being "agents of Tito."

In spite of all that, Khrushchev's criticism of Stalin was one of the most decisive upheavals in my political development.

M.G.   For me the Twentieth Congress was also a shock, but it was not something that would have meant a loss of orientation and that I therefore would have refused to accept. Khrushchev's speech helped me to establish the connection linking distinct events and phenomena. I did not perceive it as a catastrophe or as the collapse of everything that had existed up until then. On the contrary, I perceived it as the beginning of something new, as providing tremendous new opportunities for the future.

Z.M.   I completely agree with you on that. But for me personally, after Khrushchev's criticism of Stalin the question of my own responsibility began to be sharply posed. Not for what Stalin had done. I did not feel that I was personally responsible for that. But for the fact that I hadn't taken much interest in what my party was actually doing, although I was a conscious member of that party. It was after Stalin's death of course that I began to feel a presentiment that something fundamental had to change. But I did not concern myself too much about why or what would have to change. If I had had a deeper sense of personal responsibility, a great deal might have become clear to me even before it was stated by Khrushchev.

What did become clear to me was that up until that time I had been looking at everything from a point of view that for me was very convenient. My thinking was this: the party functions in the spirit of carrying out the objective laws of history, and if I conduct myself in accordance with party ideology, then I personally bear no responsibility for my political actions. The party—or better yet, history—bears that responsibility. And now suddenly Khrushchev was placing responsibility on Stalin as a specific individual, even though he was the embodiment of the party and of Communist ideology. In that case, what was I? Didn't I have personal responsibility even in cases where I thought I was acting merely in accordance with scientific ideology and the laws of history?

I experienced all this questioning not simply as something abstract but as part of my daily life. After graduation I was assigned to the Chief Prosecutor's Office in Prague, but at that office there were people who had taken part in the recent political trials, just as there were in all the top institutions of the judicial system. And from my conversations with those people I suddenly realized that they had known what they were doing: they had studied and learned by heart their roles as prosecutors and judges, according to a scenario given to them by the state security agencies with the authorization of the Political Bureau of the Communist Party of Czechoslovakia. And they knew that the defendants had learned their parts in exactly the same way. That all of it was a staged theatrical production for political purposes, not a genuine investigation and judicial process. They also knew that the defendants had been tortured. For myself I could draw only one conclusion: "My God," I thought, "these people have personal responsibility for all that!"

I found myself in great conflict because of this, and in October 1956 I transferred from the Prosecutor's Office to the Academy of Sciences. After the suppression of the Hungarian uprising at the end of 1956 many people were getting ready to take reprisals and again all the screws were being tightened. But here, too, it was precisely Moscow University that saved me from any such reprisals: after all I was a "cadre from Moscow." Nevertheless, it was written in my personnel file that since I had come from a society that was already socialist, I tended to underestimate the class struggle in less developed Czechoslovakia and tried in a mechanical way to "transfer the Soviet experience" to my own country. This charge was absolutely absurd, of course, but that's the way it was in real life.

M.G.   Yes, I remember a letter you wrote at the time; it was an entire notebook. I didn't have such dramatic conflicts then. I wasn't troubled by the question of personal responsibility in that sense, because I really didn't feel that I was responsible for any of the evils that had been committed. The main thing for me at that time was the sense of hope being born. I was working on the staff of the Young Communist League in Stavropol, and I tried to function in such a way as to arouse people's interest and activism. I organized a discussion club for young people. There was a great deal of interest, and we had to rent larger and larger meeting rooms in order to fit everyone that wanted to attend. This success and the feeling that people were waking up, as though they were being released from shackles that had bound them and were beginning to lose the sense of fear and lack of self-confidence— I was completely inspired by such things at the time. By comparison with today's standards it was rather banal, but back then it was quite an extraordinary development.

Z.M.   I understand. But if we wanted to briefly summarize what socialism meant to us in those days, even after the denunciation of Stalin, it should be said that we had not transcended the framework of the previously existing conception: for us socialism was the anticapitalist system in the USSR and in several other countries where Communist parties had come to power, as well as, in a very specific form, in Yugoslavia.

M.G.   For us young Soviet Communists there was a lot of hope at that time that everything would change in the direction of greater openness and democracy. But the thought that we were traveling on the wrong road, that it was necessary to change the whole system of economic and political relations down to their very foundations—there was no such concept.

2. NEW HOPES AND NEW DISAPPOINTMENTS

The Times Gave Birth to Optimism

z.m.   I think that the first ten years after Stalin's death had a much greater effect on both our lives than we realized at the time. I see two reasons for this. We went from the university lecture hall into practical life, and that is always a time when a person goes through the process of completing his or her formation as an individual. The overall situation at the same time aroused hope that new conceptions would actually be implemented. The so-called socialist world looked impressive. It extended from Prague through Moscow to Peking. There was the revolution in Cuba and the worldwide Communist movement. The first ventures into space were occurring, and the first man in space was a citizen of the USSR. Both the West and East were in the powerful grip of belief in the scientific and technological revolution, and it seemed that in this very sphere of endeavor the advantages of the planned economy would make themselves evident. The belief that after overcoming Stalinism, socialism would realize all its potential—that did not by any means seem as absurd to us as it does to new generations today.

m.g.   Yes, many people were inspired, not just you and I. We were ardent supporters of Khrushchev's policies. Khrushchev won a great deal of sympathy with his democratic manner, his seeming to be a man of the people [in contrast to Stalin's aloofness], with the reforms that he began, and with the revising of old ideas. The situation changed when both in politics and in economics, and in party matters, elements of voluntarism, or willfulness, appeared, a tendency to rush first in one direction, then another; also, intolerance, and sometimes outright arbitrariness and eccentricity.

z.m.   Yes, but now after the experience of perestroika we both understand all that in a different way than we did back then.

M.G.   Recently the Gorbachev Foundation held a scholarly conference in connection with the centenary of Khrushchev's birth. The participants agreed that for all his contradictory policies, the services Khrushchev rendered as a reformer were indeed great. He was the first to condemn Stalinism. But he had his limits, which he was unable to transcend. At first, as I have said, Khrushchev's policies aroused great hopes in me. In literature there was "the thaw." There was an easing of the situation in the countryside, the beginning of a new economic policy, relaxation of tensions in the international situation, the idea of peaceful coexistence, and the end to the war in Korea. All of that promised big changes. At first Khrushchev enjoyed tremendous authority. But the system resisted change. And when the reforms got into tight straits and began to be accompanied by instability in society and increased discontent, Khrushchev began to rush back and forth in different directions in search of measures to save the day and in the process committed errors and made miscalculations. Not only in domestic policy but also in foreign policy. He quarreled with the intelligentsia [who previously had sympathized with him]. And all this resulted in Khrushchev's removal. This was taken as an inevitability both in the CPSU and in the country as a whole. I also took what happened in essentially the same way and failed to understand fully the dramatic reality of what had happened.

Z.M.   I observed this about you when we met in Stavropol in 1967. We can talk more about that later on. For myself I should say that my development during those years was to a significant extent different from yours because I entered the Academy of Sciences as a result of the conflicts I experienced in the Chief Prosecutor's Office. This allowed me to continue to engage in scholarly research: for three years I read books—the classics that Professor Kechekyan had told us about in his lectures, but not only those books; also polemical works by Marxists, including works by the so-called revisionists and renegades, such figures, for example, as Trotsky. Therefore, what I saw in Khrushchev's policies of that time were certain general features, a tendency to seek some kind of new conception of socialism. That is what I saw,

rather than the shortcomings of his practical policies. Khrushchev's
main contribution and its most general significance, as I saw it, was
above all the fact that in the party program he linked the development
of socialism and communism with the scientific and technological revolution on the one hand and with ideas of a "state of the whole people"
on the other, replacing a class dictatorship with ideas of social self-
management, and so forth. I know that this was mainly on paper, but
for me these concepts on paper were obviously of very great importance when engaging in theoretical reflections on socialism. If that aspect of things had not already existed under Khrushchev, I would
hardly have arrived at the political conceptions I did in 1968.

There were two other things in the Khrushchev era that influenced
me very greatly: I visited Yugoslavia twice, and so I had the opportunity then, although quite a fleeting one, to see the "socialism of self-
management" firsthand. And I visited the West, Belgium and Italy twice.
It may sound ridiculous now, but at that time the visit to Expo-1958 [in
Brussels] was for me literally the opening of a "window on the world."

Removing Deformations and Replacing Official Cadres

M.G.   We were convinced in those days that the main thing was to
overcome the deformations in socialism and that the key to that was
to find new cadres. Along with many representatives of the new generation, I thought that in this way we could fundamentally change the
situation in our country. But when you came to visit in Stavropol in
1967 it was already clear to me that Brezhnev was not in the mood to
change cadres in any fundamental way. Matters were limited to the
mere replacement of those whose personal loyalties were not satisfactory. There was a war among different groupings going on within the
leadership itself. There was a widespread opinion in the party that
Brezhnev was just a transitory figure and that after him there would
occur a change of generations in the leadership. That is what we
thought, and of course we considered ourselves to be the generation
that would replace the older cadres and continue the reforms. But as
time went on Brezhnev strengthened his positions. And as he became

more entrenched the situation both in the CPSU and in the country as a whole changed for the worse, especially as regards democracy. Creative thinking, attempts to improve things, even simply independent opinions began to be suppressed. Gradually the reformist decisions of the plenary session of the party Central Committee in December 1965 were reduced to nothing. Those had to do with the agrarian sector. The reforms instituted by Kosygin also began to be stifled. Those reforms had sought to overcome the super-centralized administrative-command system of management of the Soviet economy. Step by step Stalinism was being revived.

z.m.   It must be acknowledged that the placing of all bets on a change of official cadres played a big role in theoretical reflections on the further possibilities for the development of socialism. We who were engaged in scholarly research and the study of political systems were also waiting impatiently for new cadres to enter politics. And they actually did in our country in 1968, and I was one of them. Aside from everything else this was because not one of the countries in the Soviet bloc at that time had experienced anything of the kind. Yet it all ended tragically.

m.g.   With all the tremendous differences what is common in our experiences is that success was impossible without changes in the center of power—in Moscow. I considered it possible to achieve such change through a replacement of cadres in the leadership.

z.m.   I could not make that same statement literally because in Czechoslovakia in 1968 an attempt to change the system had already taken place, which we will talk about further later on. But you were right that if the leadership in Moscow viewed the entire "socialist commonwealth" as merely a bunch of provinces under its control, then the system could not be changed from Prague anymore than it could from Stavropol.

m.g.   I can state with certainty that we did not understand the need to change the system and did not estimate highly enough what Khrushchev had done and what later on disappeared with him. With the advent of Brezhnev there gradually occurred a transfer of power to those who had an interest in restoring essentially the old order, although of course without the harshest methods of Stalinism: mass repression and political trials.

z.m.   For me that was one of the most fatal errors in our lifetime. I myself believed, and I tried to convince others of this in Prague at the time, that Brezhnev was just a transitory figure, that after him would come a new generation that would think the same way we did. I told myself that when people came to power in the CPSU who were like you it would be possible to have mutual understanding and real collaboration. But that all got dragged out and postponed for approximately twenty years, and after all that it was no longer possible to return to what had been torn up and crushed to pieces.

I think that I myself did not correctly evaluate the importance of two chief factors: Soviet military intervention in Hungary and the programmatic demand to "catch up with and surpass America," which was proclaimed without any clear understanding of what that would have to mean for a system of the Soviet type.

m.g.   I personally have also had to pay dearly for the views that developed within me during the Khrushchev era. As late as 1985 when I already held the highest party post I believed in the decisive significance of a change of cadres at the center and in the local areas, along with a simultaneous acceleration of scientific and technical progress.

Tanks in Budapest

z.m.   I must confess that when Soviet tanks suppressed the uprising in Hungary in the fall of 1956, in general I was not opposed to it. To be more precise, I agreed with it in principle because I was afraid that victory by the insurgents would be a real threat to socialism not only in Hungary but in our country, too, and throughout the Soviet bloc. At the same time I still looked at Hungary partially as an ally of Germany during World War II and I understood the uprising as an attempt to change something about the outcome of the war. This also played the main role for me in 1953 during the Berlin events, when I also agreed with Soviet military intervention. After all, only about ten years had elapsed then since the end of the war.

The main thing, however, was my conviction that socialism coincided with the system that predominated in Hungary (as well as in our country and in the USSR) and if the cause of socialism was being threatened, then there was nothing else to do but defend it. Although there was nothing in Czechoslovakia at that time that would have caused me to fear that such an uprising might also be possible in our country, unconsciously I was not completely confident on that score. After all, working in the prosecutor's office, I had a fairly concrete idea of why certain people in our country would have been glad to see secret police agents and some Communists hanging from the lampposts. At the same time, however, I believed that forces that were really counterrevolutionary would not try to make a move in our country. Unconsciously my lack of confidence on this score was reflected once in my dreams. I dreamed that Soviet tanks also appeared in the streets of Prague. I ran toward them and saw you in the command tower of the first tank, and I cried out, "Misha, don't shoot! It's your own people!" That's how deeply everything was all mixed together in my thinking and my feelings. My belief in socialism, doubts rising on the basis of what I knew about Stalinism, doubts that I tried to suppress within myself, and on the other hand, belief in the possibility that people like you and I under conditions of friendship and mutual understanding could change everything.

Today when I remember all that it seems absolutely clear that that was a logical position for people who belonged to the elite holding political power. We identified ourselves completely with the interests of the ruling party, whose power was being threatened.

M.G. Our views took shape also of course under the influence of the Cold War, a time when our thinking went like this: a class war is under way, the West is obviously trying to turn history back, and we need to defend ourselves. In my case, however, my understanding of the Hungarian events went through two stages. At first I perceived them as you did: we have to defend socialism, and this is a real counterrevolution. Later there came into my hands certain books, special editions put out by our own government, about the Hungarian events. They were written with a particular aim in mind. But this was done in such a way that it aroused an inner feeling of protest within me and gave rise to doubts.

Z.M.   In this regard the two of us were not exceptions. On the contrary, we were in line with the entire world Communist movement. It can't be forgotten that Khrushchev did not take the steps he did only on his own initiative; actually he consulted personally with Tito and with Mao Zedong, using Liu Shaoqi as an intermediary, as well as with Gomulka in Poland. It was not only the leaders of the Communist parties in power who agreed with the military intervention but also the Communist parties of Italy, France, and other countries. That is, this included representatives of tendencies that even then might have been called reformist and that had a certain independence from Moscow.

After the military intervention the most convincing position for me was the Yugoslav one formulated by Edvard Kardelj in a lengthy article. His main argument was that after the suppression of the counterrevolution it was not possible to restore the old system in the form that had brought about the crisis, but it was necessary to support aspirations toward the development of self-managed socialism. After all, during the uprising there were not only anti-Communist combat groups operating in Budapest but also workers councils at the main factories. I agreed with Kardelj that the Yugoslav model of that time was better, because the crisis and uprising had been caused by Stalinism under the Hungarian Communist Party leader Rakosi. Thanks to that article I learned to read Serbo-Croatian and began to take a more serious interest in the Yugoslav model, of which I was then a supporter. But this happened a few years later, as did my attempts to work in favor of reform within the Communist Party of Czechoslovakia. In 1959 I was still speaking publicly in the opposite direction, criticizing "revisionism," including the Yugoslav variety. But I will tell more about that later on. The point is that at the end of 1956 two different positions were already interwoven in my thinking, and at that time they didn't seem to me mutually exclusive.

On the one hand, socialism was for me a system that existed only in countries where the Communist parties had taken power. On the other, I leaned toward the point of view that within this framework various models—or, as was said at the time, various roads to socialism—were possible. Among those, the model I sympathized with the most was the Yugoslav model of "self-managed socialism."

At that time I didn't take into account the factor of military force. Only later, after 1968 in fact, I realized how profoundly mistaken I was on this point—precisely because I hadn't seen that these positions were mutually exclusive—even though military intervention in Hungary in 1956 had clearly shown that. Because if the question of the admissibility of any specific road to socialism could be decided in the last analysis by military force, then whoever lacked sufficient military force would have no real possibility to choose. Even the real influence of the ruling Communist parties was a derivative of the strength of the armies they commanded. On this basis, it could also happen that socialism as a factor in international politics might be reduced to the question of military power and consequently the arms race could legitimately be presented as a form of the class struggle. On the basis of this kind of thinking one could never break free from the sorcerer's spell of the Cold War.

M.G.   Now we are already approaching the question of a break with the old way of thinking and the emergence of the new thinking in international and domestic politics after 1985.

The Meaning of the Slogan "Catch Up With and Surpass the West"

Z.M.   Today, after all that we have lived through, and after the disintegration of the Soviet system, I return in my thoughts to the views we held in the Khrushchev era that socialism would develop into com-

munism when a scientific and technological base was built that was of
a higher quality than that in the advanced capitalist countries. Today
that programmatic thesis seems to me quite contradictory.

This is something that I personally—back then, around 1960—did
not understand. I have in mind the following problem: to put it briefly,
Stalin never permitted comparisons of socialism or communism with
capitalist reality because he argued that an entirely new world was
being built here that could not be compared with any preceding system.
This of course resulted in isolation from "the rest of the world," but
in a way it had its own logic: Our successes could be measured only
by our own standards of measurement, which corresponded to our
own Communist ideology. In what respect people in the West lived
better than we did, in what respect the same, and in what respect
worse—all that was unimportant. Khrushchev, with his slogan "Catch
up with and surpass America," changed the situation fundamentally
for the ordinary Soviet citizen. It's as though he were saying that now
the aim was to live the way they do over there, and in a certain sense
to live even better, in accordance with communist principles. After that,
over the course of many long years, a comparison was indeed made,
and entire generations of young people became convinced that in fact
the standard of living of Americans was incomparably higher than
ours. Whoever searched for the reason for this might easily come to
the conclusion that the main obstacle was the existing economic and
political system. That is, the opposite of what Khrushchev intended
occurred. He wanted to strengthen people's faith in the Soviet system,
but in fact the practical comparison with the West had the opposite
effect and constantly weakened that faith. In the end most Soviet citizens lost this faith entirely, and the young generation simply didn't have
it anymore.

In order for the Soviet system in general to stand up and justify itself
in such a competition, it would have had to reform itself in a fundamental way into a different kind of system that would have allowed
various individuals to operate autonomously, not only in economics
but also in political life. Consequently, it was necessary to give free
reign to the market and to democracy. It was approximately principles

such as this that became the broadest basis for the conceptions of economic and political reform in the Prague Spring of 1968. Did you encounter this kind of problem under the conditions you lived in, in your party work of that time? If so, when and how?

M.G.   Yes, of course. Above all, people began to understand that these programmatic slogans were basically empty declarations. They soon became an object of ridicule in all strata of our society and within the party itself. The damage done to the authority of the CPSU and to socialism was colossal. I remember an anecdote from that time. A certain lecturer, speaking about future communist society, concluded with the following remarks, "The breaking day of communism is already visible, gleaming just over the horizon." At this point an old peasant who had been sitting in the front row stood up and asked, "Comrade Lecturer, what is a horizon?" The lecturer explained that it is a line where the earth and the sky seem to meet, having the unique characteristic that the more you move toward it, the more it moves away. The old peasant responded: "Thank you, Comrade Lecturer. Now everything is quite clear."

But you're right that a comparison between programmatic declarations and real life was bound to lead, and in fact did lead, to reflections on the lack of efficiency in our economic and political system. Both Khrushchev himself and many others after him made stubborn attempts to reform both the economic and the political system, but they took only half-measures. They couldn't have done anything more. I understand that quite well now. But in life at that time such efforts developed into genuine dramas. People who showed initiative could not break out of the trap that the system confronted them with.

When I was still working in Stavropol I constantly encountered the fact that when local officials took selfless actions seeking to modernize industry or introduce new technology to make people's work easier or to reorganize life in a better way for city dwellers or rural residents— they always came into conflict with the law.

One particular episode comes to mind. The chairman of the collective farm in one of the districts of Stavropol demonstrated an irrigation system that had produced magnificent crops of both grain and fodder. I said I was very pleased by this, but at the same time I asked, "Where did you get the pipe to do this irrigation? After all, pipe can only be obtained according to the plan." The man I was talking with only smiled. At that time I was secretary of the Stavropol territory party committee, a member of the Central Committee of the CPSU, and a deputy to the Supreme Soviet, but all I could do was smile along with him, because I understood the whole absurdity of the situation. It was obvious to both of us that he had to "arrange something," to work around the existing system, in order to obtain the necessary pipe. The system held everyone firmly in its grip, stifling initiative. In order to protect itself, it suppressed both freedom of thought and any kind of searching or exploration.

z.m.   Out of all this, however, there grew up, over the course of the entire twenty-year period after the Khrushchev era, a certain system of relations in which the official mode of existence for society, its norms and ways of governing people, diverged more and more from reality. In everyday practice people more and more frequently acted, and simply had to act, differently from the way they were told to—as the example of your collective farm chairman demonstrates. They acted according to the rules of their own common sense, one might say. As a result of all this there grew up what it has already become accepted to call a shadow economy, another separate sector of the economy. But this was true not only in economic life; it applied to the actual way people behaved in all areas of life.

This was a living reality, although officially it remained in the shadows; it kept growing stronger and stronger, and its needs or requirements became the actual content of the reforms when they began to be implemented once again. So in this sense Nikita Khrushchev's main contribution was something that he himself didn't intend: he became the initiator of a process of development which destroyed the original Stalinist system but with results substantially different from those laid out in the 1961 program of the CPSU. I myself would never have supposed this back at the time when that program inspired me in the direction of reform politics. It was only many years later that I under-stood all this.

M.G.   What you called the "shadow reality" was actually normal, everyday human life, a way of escaping from the situation. By this I do not mean to justify the activity of criminal elements involved in the shadow economy. Everything is clear with regard to that. The system that was established in our country under Stalin, and that was later preserved with some changes, was a system for mobilizing society un-der extreme conditions. It was not appropriate for normal everyday life. But unless people are forced to do otherwise by revolutions, wars, or other catastrophes, they want to live a normal life and therefore this system was eventually bound to collapse.

3. TWENTY YEARS, DIVERGENT PATHS

Z.M.   This part of our conversation will be a little different in form. It will consist of short monologues, one following the other. Because now we are talking about a twenty-year period in which we did not see each other, a time when we were following such different paths that each of us needs to speak only about the path he was following inde-pendently.

With a Soviet Submachine Gun at Our Backs

Z.M.   Right now I'm not going to talk about my concepts of reform socialism which I sought to implement in 1968. We are sure to discuss that more than once later on in connection with our understanding of socialism. I also do not want to, nor could I, describe in detail the whole history that culminated in my being shipped off to the Kremlin, where there took place a humiliating ceremony of capitulation by our country, although it was called "negotiations in the Kremlin." I only want to say briefly that in the early morning hours of August 21, 1968, a report came that Soviet troops had invaded Czechoslovakia. The collapse of my political world then was more terrible than any of the previous political shocks I had experienced.

On the one hand, I was suddenly seized by the irresistible thought that all of my Communist convictions, from which I had derived the strength and determination to pursue the reforms that I was trying to carry out through the ruling Communist Party, suddenly seemed to me naive stupidity. You're just a fool, I said to myself. On the other hand, I knew that something had to be done at that moment, something that would prevent senseless bloodshed. What that might be, what might turn out to be possible and what would not be possible, I simply did not know. But in the end a person comes to know such things in politics only through the course of events. Nevertheless, I was convinced that we could not try to offer military resistance. The superiority was so clearly on the Soviet side. And it occurred to me that some people in the Kremlin might be hoping precisely that we would offer resistance in order subsequently to be able to assert, as in the case of Hungary in 1956, that it was a counterrevolutionary armed uprising and that, therefore, Soviet tanks were necessary to defend socialism.

We—some members of the party's leadership, to which I also belonged at that time—were in a conference room together with Dubček, [Alexander Dubček was the head of the Czechoslovak Communist Party at the time of the Prague Spring] when bursting into the room there came soldiers of the Soviet Taman division and one of them took his place behind each of us and aimed a Kalashnikov submachine gun at our backs. One's concept of socialism at such a moment moves to last place, but unconsciously at the same time you know that it has a direct connection of some sort with the automatic weapon pointing at your back.

Everything that followed, including the fact that in Moscow I signed the so-called Moscow Protocol and why I did that, is recounted in detail in my memoir *Nightfrost in Prague* [New York: Karz Publishers, 1980]. Under the guise of a "policy of normalization" neo-Stalinist practices were gradually restored in Czechoslovakia, something that already prevailed in the USSR and with varying degrees of deviation in all of the Soviet bloc. From the point of view of those who imposed these practices, the so-called Prague Spring was truly a departure from the norm, and they wanted to stop Czechoslovakia from being different from the other socialist countries—that is, they wanted to "normalize everything" in that sense, to serve their own advantage.

In November 1968 I resigned from all the party posts I held because my initial thinking was that, even after the Soviet intervention and the signing of the so-called Moscow Protocol, it would still be possible to preserve something in the way of reform policies, but that turned out to be a further illusion. After that you could say that I disappeared from the scene. I no longer attended Central Committee meetings of the Communist Party of Czechoslovakia. Not even the one in September 1969 where I was expelled from that body. In March 1970 I was expelled from the party almost exactly a quarter of a century after I had joined it.

I viewed all this as a kind of logical consequence of the fact that the attempt to reform the system—and I belonged to the group of intellectual and political initiators of that attempt—had been defeated precisely in the way it was, that is, by armies and tanks. From this new experience there began for me a further process of development in my understanding of socialism. I no longer identified socialism with the system existing in the USSR. And not only because Soviet tanks had been sent against our policies of reform. At various Central Committee sessions during 1968, as I came to know the form and method of thinking on the part of Brezhnev, Suslov, and other old-timers in Moscow, and not only theirs but also the thinking of Gomulka, Ulbricht, and Zhivkov [the Communist leaders of Poland, East Germany, and Bulgaria respectively] I simply began to lose the ability to believe that as long as these men represented the ruling parties, those parties would be capable of reforming anything.

I withdrew far away from politics, isolated myself among the beetles in the National Museum, because entomology was my hobby and as a young man I had wanted to take that up as a profession.

In January 1969 a long period began during which I was to learn how the party dealt with those it didn't like. The paradox was that the so-called Moscow Protocol ensured me a special place among the so-called enemies of socialism. To the best of my knowledge, the leadership of the CPC was not allowed, without Moscow's consent, to decide the fate of those whose signatures were on that document. After all, Brezhnev's signature came first on that document, and in all likelihood he remembered that it had often been a risky business in the history of his own party when one's signature appeared in the company of other signatures belonging to condemned "enemies of the people." I think that prevented some people who were especially zealous in Prague from throwing me in prison. Then one day in November 1969 I was sitting in the museum—in the frame of mind that I've described at that time— and I saw in the newspaper a headline saying "M.S. Gorbachev in Prague." I must admit to you that the first thing that occurred to me was that you had come as a member of that delegation in order to meet with me.

For me, a person who had just been expelled from the Central Committee, it was no longer possible to try and seek you out through official channels. I tried to do it through people I knew in the party apparatus. They told me that your delegation had just left Prague, but as soon as it returned they would let me know. But no one ever did let me know.

M.G.   I did ask about you of course. In general I was told the same thing, that you "weren't in Prague." But a member of the Czech leadership, Alois Indra himself, showed me quite eagerly an office in the building of the CPC Cenral Committee and said, "This is where Zdeněk used to sit." It was a surprise to me to be included in that delegation. I hadn't known anything about it in advance and was unprepared for it. The Prague leadership was having great difficulties with young people. A request had come to Moscow to send a delegation of those who had experience working in the Young Communist League, and that's why the choice fell on me among others. We did come to Czechoslovakia, and that had far-reaching consequences for me. With my own eyes I saw that the people did not accept what had happened in August 1968. In the city of Brno we visited a defense plant, the so-called Zbrojevka. But no contact with the workers resulted: people turned their backs on us; they didn't want to speak with us. This was repeated in Bratislava; there too we found ourselves isolated. For me this was a shock. I suddenly understood that despite all the global, strategic, and ideological justifications, we had suppressed something that had grown up within our own society. From that time on I began to think more and more about our own situation and I came to rather unconsoling conclusions—that something wasn't right among us.

This happened not only in my case. The intervention in Czechoslovakia caused a great many doubts in the USSR, including among Communists. There were quite a few who openly condemned the intervention, and I must admit that before that [before the 1969 trip to Czechoslovakia], I myself, as secretary of the Stavropol territorial committee of the party, took part indirectly in an attempt to contain rising criticism in regard to the Czechoslovak events.

Z.M.   And wasn't I an outright "enemy of the people"?

M.G.   No, I always said openly that I could not agree that Zdeněk was any kind of counterrevolutionary.

Z.M.   I think I understand your situation, Misha. I have already mentioned that I myself in 1959 took part in a "struggle against revisionism" even though at that time I considered many of the views held by the Yugoslav Communists to be correct. But if I had declared that openly, my political role in the CPC in 1968 would not have been possible. I think that things like this lead many people to an oversimplified conclusion—that politics is simply a kind of swinishness. An acquaintance of mine spent a lot of time working on his cottage in the country trying to clean a wall by removing layer after layer of material that had accumulated on it. And once the wall had been completely cleaned it fell down. He said that's the same way it is in politics. Everything is held together by some kind of grime and muck. In politics such things can't be completely avoided, but it is necessary to try not to get muddied up more than is acceptable from the standpoint of ordinary human decency.

A Socialist, and Therefore a Dissident and Émigré

z.m. When I withdrew into the silence of those museum collections
I gave myself five years to stay out of politics. After all, the result of
my efforts had also been that now the Soviet army was in our country
and the political situation was much worse than before those efforts.
I did not blame myself for the decision made in the Kremlin, but I
thought then, as I still do now, that good intentions by themselves do
not free a person from responsibility. And so I thought it was proper
to stay out of politics for a while and not to interfere with what was
being done by those who took the wheel after the collapse of my policies. After the experience of the Hungarian events five years seemed
to be an appropriate length of time. It was not until 1961 that Kádár
began a certain change of policy under the slogan "Whoever is not
against us is with us." And I still believed in the possibility of a certain
"Kadarization" in Czechoslovakia. Therefore, until 1973 I could not
be considered one of the dissidents, because I held my tongue. Only
after that did I begin to sign various petitions of protest against political
repression, and so forth.

Unlike in Hungary, in our country no relaxation of repression occurred. On the contrary, thousands of highly qualified people could
not find work in their profession in any kind of responsible position,
not to speak of the total ban on such people working in science, in
higher education, or in the press. In Western Europe at the same time
so-called Euro-Communism was flourishing successfully as the leading
Communist parties of Western Europe, the Italian, French, Spanish,
and British parties openly proclaimed themselves supporters of the
Prague Spring and condemned Soviet military intervention. A conference of representatives of European Communist parties was scheduled
to be held in Berlin in 1976. The Soviet leadership also had an interest,
although from the outside, in a successful conclusion of this conference. Therefore, in early 1975 I wrote an extensive analysis of theoretical questions and discussion of the practical course of the Prague
Spring in a way that I thought would be acceptable above all for the
Euro-Communists but with the aim also of making it acceptable for

representatives of some other parties, for example, the Hungarian, Polish, and Romanian. I sent this document to the Central Committees of all the parties that were to participate in the conference and consequently to the Central Committees of the CPSU and the CPC.

The response came very quickly in the form of a group of state security agents who broke into my apartment at 5:00 in the morning and carried out a search. The big "find" that they carried away was the manuscript that the Central Committee of the CPC had already received by mail. From then on I became the object of constant surveillance as well as acts of provocation by the state security agency. The official Communist Party refused to engage my criticism in any way other than by police methods. However, this resulted over the course of time in bringing all critically minded people very close together, people of the most different origins and tendencies. Reform Communists began to meet not only with Social Democrats and liberals but also with Catholics and other religious dissidents. Over the course of time it became clear to everyone that without basic civil rights, especially freedom of belief and freedom of opinion, neither Catholics nor socialists could accomplish anything.

This was a time, not long after the 1975 Helsinki conference on security and cooperation in Europe, when all the countries of the Soviet bloc were also ratifying international treaties on human rights. This was the basis on which a human rights movement began to develop, most often in the form of so-called Helsinki committees. It was no longer possible to fight against this movement with Stalinist methods of mass arrest or even execution, and therefore people who were willing to live with discrimination and other forms of repression were able to engage in critical or oppositional activity in the Soviet bloc. Such activity was highly variegated as far as the goals and views of the participants, and therefore the vague and general term "dissident movement" was used to designate such activity. In 1976 in Czechoslovakia a platform for civil liberties and human rights was drawn up. We called it Charter 77 [a kind of Magna Carta to be introduced in the year 1977]. I was one of the initiators of Charter 77, and half of the first 240 "signatories" were reform Communists. To this day I think that it was precisely this unification of various democratic-minded trends of opinion that frightened the political leadership in Prague to such an extent that, along with an unparalleled propaganda campaign, there began acts of repression, including arrest and imprisonment. That is what happened very soon to the noted liberal intellectual and playwright Václav Havel. Today he's the president of the Czech Republic, but at that time he ended in prison, as did the reform Communist journalist Jiří Dienstbier, who later became Czech foreign minister from 1989 to 1992. In addition to them, there was a confirmed Marxist of Trotskyist persuasion, Petr Uhl, who later, in 1990, was for a short time director of the Czechoslovak Press Agency and who today has again become a critic of certain aspects of the new regime. There were many other less famous dissidents.

After the publication of Charter 77, I was dismissed from my job at the museum and in effect placed under house arrest. Police sat outside the doors of our apartment around the clock, accompanied me wherever I went, and checked the identification papers of everyone I met when I was out or everyone who came to our home. The result was that I was completely isolated and faced the prospect of having to earn my living by manual labor. At the same time there was an official proposal that I go abroad. I was nearly fifty years old, we only live once, and I had no desire to play the role of political martyr. Therefore, after a while, I accepted this proposal, and in June 1977 I emigrated to Vienna. The Austrian chancellor at that time was the Social Democratic leader Bruno Kreisky, and he had promised to grant political asylum to anyone who was forced to emigrate from Czechoslovakia for having signed the Charter 77 document.

Once I was in exile, and as time went on, I returned to the kind of work I had been engaged in for so long before 1968 at the Academy of Sciences in Prague—theoretical analysis of systems of the Soviet type. The concept of socialism became part of the content of my professional work as a political scientist. At the same time I did not abandon my critical activity in relation to the regime in Prague and in the Soviet bloc in general, and my articles opposing the so-called policy of normalization, if gathered together, would make up a fairly substantial volume.

On the whole I can only say I am grateful in the final analysis to both Brezhnev and Husák [Gustáv Husák was the leader of the Czechoslovak Communist Party imposed after the Soviet invasion]—I am grateful to them for the fact that I did not have to live within their former sphere of influence for a period of twenty years. I do not feel as though twenty years of my life had been stolen from me, as do many of my friends, who lived all that time inside Czechoslovakia. Moreover, from the experience of life in the West I came to understand what social democratic reformism means, that it is an orientation generally to the left of contemporary West European society, and I also came to understand the point of view of this society toward problems of the so-called Third World, global ecological problems, and so forth.

In fact, I do consider myself a person of left orientation, a socialist whose views willy-nilly were formed under the impact, on the one hand, of a life experience that was contradictory but certainly not impoverished and, on the other, under the impact of an education whose starting point was the philosophy of Marxism.

From the Provinces to the Kremlin

M.G. As I've already said, the Czechoslovakia of 1968 was for me a major impulse toward critical thinking. I understood that there was something in our country that was not right. But this impulse came from the outside world. In 1970 I became first secretary of the Stavropol territorial committee of the Communist Party, and my knowledge both about our society and about the functioning of the Central Committee and the government was greatly expanded. I have written in detail about that time in several chapters of my memoirs. For now let me just say that I gradually, and more and more tangibly, discovered that although I held positions of high authority, in fact there was little I could do, because I was bound hand and foot by orders from the center.

You know perhaps better than others that by my very nature I was always drawn toward radicalism and democracy. It was always that way. The style of work I developed in Stavropol corresponded to that. But that style of work was not considered acceptable; it was not the stereotypical way in which leadership cadre were supposed to behave. And sometimes I simply had to break myself of a habit, what I was used to doing normally. From my own experience I could see how difficult it was, and most often how impossible it was, to change either the forms or the principles of economic activity either in industry or in agriculture. All eyes were fixed on the center, and it rejected any kind of innovation, or else it drained the energy and vitality out of any kind of initiative. My first doubts about the effectiveness of the system were born at that time. My trips to other parts of the country and contacts with colleagues showed me that the same kinds of problems were tormenting them. The most "experienced" party secretaries adapted to the peculiarities of the system. It was necessary for me also to take their experience into account. Both the general secretary at the center and the various first secretaries in the regions repaid support with protection. This hierarchy of vassals and chiefs of principalities was in fact the way the country was run. The democratic façade did not change the essence of the matter. It was a caste system based on mutual protection. To me this was a distortion of socialism and by no means a defect inherent in that system.

z.m.   Good, that is true in general. But we both lived through a great many different things then. And for my part I cannot say that I any longer equated socialism with what existed in practice, as I had previously. Moreover, it was precisely because so many people had ceased to identify the system with the concept of socialism that the expression "actually existing socialism" was invented, because the leadership wanted to assert that its actual practice was identical with socialism. But I don't agree, incidentally, that it was simpler for me and for people in Czechoslovakia in general, because awareness was supposedly brought by Soviet tanks to those who for a long time had remained true believers. Supposedly this was a personal gift from Brezhnev to open our eyes.

M.G.   At a certain stage my concepts of socialism began to diverge [from officially approved concepts], along with the requirements of life itself. First of all, this had to do with democracy. Probably the roots of the slogan that arose in the first years of perestroika, "more democracy, more socialism," can be found here. Even before perestroika, under Chernenko, I stressed the idea of the important role of the human factor. All this amounted to exploratory attempts to answer questions being given birth by life itself. We had had absolutely no experience of democracy, and what came from abroad was regarded as alien and unacceptable. In your case, even before the 1970s you began to think about the need to change the system, but at that time I could not say such a thing about myself. To be sure, I was overflowing with impressions from my experiences, reflections, questions. But everything remained within a closed circle for me, and the only way out that I could see was a fundamental change of personnel—everything depended on people. Working in Stavropol, I tried to put these conclusions of mine into practice. I tried to open the way for people of the younger generation in my activities, people for whom traditional stereotypes, hypocrisy, and practice of the double standard were unacceptable, including proclamations by *nomenklatura* officials of principles for other people which they did not live by themselves. I considered it my duty to support whatever was new and to encourage the development of a democratic atmosphere in our region. Today someone might look back with a mocking smile and evaluate my activities in that period as follows: "Gorbachev," they might say, "wanted to create a Stavropol with a human face." But I was behaving like a typical believer in enlightenment—new educated people would come along and change everything.

In the 1970s, thanks to the privilege that members of the Central Committee and first secretaries of regional committees enjoyed, I became acquainted with a different point of view toward socialism. There was a special category of people who received the so-called white books of Progress Publishers. In this way I was able to read a three-volume history of the USSR by Giuseppe Boffa (the Italian Communist historian and journalist), works by the Italian Communist Party leader Palmiro Togliatti, a collection of essays [on the Prague Spring] entitled *The Dubček Drama,* and books by Antonio Gramsci, Roger Garaudy [the French Communist theoretician], and articles by the West German Social Democratic leader Willy Brandt and the French Socialist Party leader François Mitterrand. My trips abroad were of no small importance to me, accompanied by numerous contacts, conversations, and discussions on the most varied themes.

In 1978 I was promoted to a high post as a secretary of the CPSU Central Committee, moving from the provinces to the center, to Moscow. As a Central Committee member I at first tried to continue doing what I was used to, that is, to engage in the same activities on a nationwide scale that I had in the Stavropol region. As time went by the limits of the possibilities available to me became clear, and I began to understand that the problem was not which rung of the hierarchical ladder I was standing on, but something much more complex. A turning point in my thinking essentially began in 1983, after Andropov became the head of the party. I can't go into a more detailed assessment of his activity here, nor do I wish to. Yuri Vladimirovich [Andropov] was a very interesting and complex personality. We were well acquainted from working together at an earlier time in Stavropol; he had been in our region for treatment, to take a cure. Andropov definitely wanted to start making changes, he supported the promotion of new officials, but there were certain bounds he could not go beyond; he was too deeply entrenched in his own past experience—it held him firmly in its grasp.

But the turning point in my thinking was not directly connected with the kind of ideas he had. The change came about as a result of a particular instance; on Andropov's suggestion I was assigned to give a report on the sixtieth anniversary of Lenin's death. For a long time I thought over what the central conception of this report would be, and I decided to reread Lenin's last articles. I had a desire to understand what his greatest concerns were at the time, why those final writings of his came into existence. What was the meaning of his admission that after October we took a wrong path, made a mistake, and had to fundamentally revise our point of view regarding socialism? Seeing that power was being concentrated in the hands of the Communist bureaucracy, Lenin consistently stressed the idea that socialism equals the vital, creative activity of the masses. This was Lenin returning to his own true self: the idea that the groundwork for socialism is prepared by the development of democracy and that socialism becomes a reality through democracy. The drama surrounding this man was revealed to me. Here was a revolutionary giant, a man of great culture, who ended up a captive of his own ideological constructs. At the end he was trying to break out of the closed circle of dogma encompassing him.

This was an impulse that drove me to further reflection. Even then it was my view, which became stronger and stronger, that more democracy both inside the party and in the society as a whole was what was needed to reinvigorate socialism. The possibility of a choice among various alternatives I saw as a means of providing people with the possibility of self-determination and self-realization.

z.m.   This already sounds like some of the speeches that were given during the Prague Spring in 1968, and so you and I were again starting to walk along the same road, although we would not meet for another six years, that is, in 1989.

Shared Hopes Once Again

z.m.   Misha, when you showed up in early 1985 as the head of the CPSU that meant for me that I had to explore something within myself, my own personal attitude. At that time I no longer believed it likely in general that someone might try to organize a Moscow Spring in the USSR. It seemed to me that neither the CPSU nor Soviet society were capable of that, that generational and personnel changes that would have to happen would result essentially in nothing more than technocratic attempts to improve the system, but I did not expect any attempt

to achieve "more socialism, more democracy." Nevertheless, I was convinced that in order to avoid a war, a final decision had to be made in
the USSR to overcome the totalitarian nature of political power, and
that that would happen, most likely later on, perhaps in the 1990s, but
it was impossible to foresee exactly how this would happen. I did not
wish to see any catastrophes, and so I hoped for reform, but I must
repeat, I didn't expect it along the lines of our experience of 1968.

Your arrival at the summit of political power meant that I was suddenly faced with new questions on all sides. On the whole I could
imagine—and as things turned out later this was essentially correct—
that you would strive to achieve precisely what I no longer expected.
And if after all, even with a twenty-year delay, the system in the USSR
could be reformed in the direction of linking socialism and democracy,
what then? What if I had been mistaken up until then, because my own
defeat in 1968 had given rise to pessimism instead of objectivity? With
all those doubts I felt I should immediately and publicly—in the press,
on television, in any important political consultation in general—take
a clear position [in support of Gorbachev]. At that moment I was the
only person in the West who knew you well on a personal basis, even
though it was a long time back, in our student years, that we had
known each other. Thus, not only journalists but politicians as well,
beginning with Kreisky and Brandt and ending with diplomats and
specialists in information-gathering, not only from the United States
but from China as well—all these people took an interest in consulting
with me.

So then, as early as 1985, I came to a definite conclusion that I
believed in you sufficiently that I could assert with a clear conscience
that Gorbachev would try to carry out changes of a completely principled character both internally and in foreign policy. In general I
guessed the direction of these changes, but not the pace at which developments would occur. Also, I did not guess how powerful nationalism in the USSR would turn out to be, or that the Soviet system would
fall apart before it could be reformed. But you didn't presume anything
like that either, nor did any of those who asked me about my views on
the future.

It tormented me that all this had not happened ten years earlier. I could imagine that in such a case it would have still been possible for us to turn our friendship into a political factor, to revive the ideas of 1968 in Czechoslovakia with your support. But by 1985 it was too late for that, even if I had been in Prague—leaving aside the fact that I was actually living in exile. So then, despite pressure from people around me to write you and ask to meet, I never did that. On the one hand, I thought it would be superfluous, because you yourself knew that your tanks were in Prague and that I was in Vienna and what my views were. At the same time I presumed essentially that, just as my full confidence in you remained unshaken, you also trusted me. (I was assured of that actually by Willy Brandt, after he had talked with you.) So I said to myself: "Well now, it's your turn, Misha. You have to decide when we will meet again."

Even without that I had quite a few opportunities to support your policies from the outside, which I did. In so doing I was inclined to reevaluate the concepts and ideas of the Prague Spring as a possible model for the policy of perestroika. This is evident; for example, in a series of articles I published in late 1986 in the Italian Communist weekly *Rinascita*.

M.G.   I of course knew your views and read a great deal of what you wrote, for example, the article in the Italian Communist paper *L'Unità* about our years as students together. That our friendship and mutual trust had withstood and survived all the experiences of the preceding twenty years—I was also certain of that. But at the very beginning, in 1985, I had no concept that really fundamental changes would not be possible within the framework of the system. Each of us had to follow his own difficult path to knowledge.

How We Sought to Reinvigorate Socialism

1. THE PRAGUE SPRING AND ITS DEFEAT

Socialism Must Be Linked with Democracy and the Market

z.m.   Beginning in approximately 1963, in my theoretical articles and articles on current events, I began working more systematically on questions concerning the possibility of linking socialism with democracy.

Originally I took as my starting point certain basic ideas, or "theses," put forward in Khrushchev's 1961 program of the CPSU: the so-called state of the whole people, which was supposed to take the place of the dictatorship of the proletariat; and the development of elements of social self-management. These were general notions, but if a person took them seriously and was convinced that it was correct in principle to develop Marx and Lenin's ideas, a vast number of questions could arise. I was just such a person at the time, and consequently I began to ask what all this could mean concretely for the development of the existing structures of political power, of the state, and the overall administration of society.

The first general summary of my thinking can be found in the popularized scientific booklet *The State and the Individual*, published in Prague in 1964. Some of the chapter headings were as follows: "The State and the Citizen"; "The Interests of the State and the Interests of People"; "The Individual before the Law"; "Democracy and the Economy."

At that time I came to approximately the following conclusion: democracy and socialism are more than compatible; the one is necessary to reinforce the other; they cannot be placed in opposition to one another. Under socialism, the concept of democracy must consider that citizens who are equal before the law are in reality not equal socially. Socialism must therefore bring into public life and politics not only the citizen in the abstract but the real, socially defined human being as well. This refers to the main social strata with their various interests, which may differ and conflict with one another, depending on social position, division of labor, levels of skill and education, age, gender, and so forth.

Under socialism, all the possible different interests of people should first of all be freely expressed and only then, in the democratic clash of those interests, would it be possible to seek and find interests that would be common to all and of significance to society as a whole. In order for this to become possible in general, it would be necessary not only to "grant permission" for this process to take place but also to alter the structure of the political system.

At this point I came to the conclusion that it was a mistake to deny the principles of separation of powers and a government of law, advocating instead a broader participation by working people in government administration through a "state of the Soviet type" (or historically, a "state of the type of the Paris Commune"). I concluded that a government of law, with separation of powers, was also applicable to socialism. At the same time, however, direct influence on government by the various strata of working people in society should be ensured in special ways, ways that were not known to Western parliamentary democracy. All this could take place by having social organizations assume a political role (beginning with the trade unions and ending with women's and youth organizations). But the main role in all this would be played by workers' self-management bodies in the factories, and these bodies would be raised to a level involving the government as a whole (through the establishment, for example, of separate houses of parliament for workers' councils, etc.).

As for the economy, it was necessary to overcome the system of planning by decree and to establish the socialist enterprise as an autonomous agent that would be able to enter the market in that capacity.

I myself remained at that general level of understanding of things, and as far as any specific economic conception was concerned, I referred to the theories being propounded by Ota Šik at that time. He advocated a market linked with social (governmental) regulation of certain important economic processes.

The first version of this booklet lacked a more or less integrated section on "the leading role of the Communist Party" because I myself had no clear conception of what to say about that. The fact that modern-day ideology and practice contradicted my general conceptions in this particular case was quite evident. But, first, it was impossible at that time to try to analyze openly and critically this extremely sensitive political question. And second, that could have interfered with the publication of the book. Yet really, the main thing was that I myself was not clear on how to solve this problem in a way consistent with my Communist convictions. A Central Committee secretary of the CPC, V. Koucký, advised me quite openly and with good intentions to include this topic in the book. So I added a short section about the leading role of the CPC, which contained a fundamental proposition that was later included in the CPC's Action Program. It stated the following: The Communist Party could play a leading role in ensuring democracy under socialism only under two conditions. First, if it really did unite in its ranks people who could be considered a "conscious vanguard" because they actually did subordinate in practice, not just in words, private or partial group interests to the overall interests and socialist goals of the entire society. Second, if such a party did not perceive its leadership as something to be taken for granted for all time, but instead was able to win over the majority of society again and again through tireless persuasion.

Although this went rather significantly beyond the framework of party ideology at the time, including the CPSU Program, the general level of my thinking still remained within the framework of a conception of socialism as an anti-capitalist system being built on the basis of the system of the Soviet type in the countries where Communist parties were in power.

Reforms Caused by Optimism, Not by Necessity

z.m.   I think that for me personally as well as for most reform-minded
Communists in Czechoslovakia in 1968 it was typical that we wanted
to fundamentally reform the existing system not because we felt driven
to do so by a sense of crisis. On the contrary, it seemed to us then that
a profound political crisis in the form of Stalinist domination was already behind us and that difficulties in the economic sphere could be
overcome by a market-oriented reform. The idea of "catching up with
the advanced Western countries" under such circumstances did not
seem to us a meaningless slogan. And for Czechoslovakia at that time
such an idea was not senseless: a number of economic indicators placed
us on the same level as Austria or even better. At the same time the
Czechs with their "good soldier Schweik" sense of humor were making
fun of the overblown slogan that in twenty years we would "surpass
America." There was a joke that went like this: "Why is it that the
socialist camp can catch up with America, but can't pass it? Because
we don't want the Americans to see our bare behind."

m.g.   Until now I thought that joke was a Soviet achievement.

z.m.   Even with that kind of skepticism among the people, for the
most part a sense of optimism rather than hopelessness prevailed in
our society.

However, even then this was evidently connected with rather specific
conditions in Czechoslovakia that were not repeatable in other countries of the Soviet bloc. These special conditions made it possible on
the one hand for the Prague Spring to arise and develop the way it did.
But because of these particular features the attempt at reform remained
isolated and found no continuation or further advancement in any of
the surrounding countries. I think that the following specific features
of Czechoslovak development played a primary role.

In the years 1945–48, that is before the Communist Party of
Czechoslovakia seized a monopoly of power, basic measures of so-

cialization of the economy had already been carried out. The key industrial sectors and enterprises as well as the banking industry had been nationalized. By the end of 1947 the public sector produced more than half the social product, and small business produced another quarter, and only the final quarter or less remained in the private capitalist sector. Nationalized enterprises remained independent agents on the market, without being subordinated to the commands of any planning institution or ministry. Skilled specialists directed the nationalized enterprises, but management was monitored by enterprise committees, which consisted in part of workers at the enterprise and which enjoyed substantial powers. As much as two-thirds of the national income designated for consumption went to wage workers and the remainder to handicraftsmen, independent specialists, and white-collar workers. Only 6 percent went to the capitalist sector.

On the political level a multiparty system existed along with free elections in which the Communist Party of Czechoslovakia in 1946 received more than 38 percent of the vote and together with the Social Democratic Party had an absolute majority. There was, however, a limitation on this pluralism: in contrast to Western parliamentary systems all of the existing parties (four in the Czech region and four in Slovakia) participated in a coalition that bore the name National Front, and they all took part in the government. The general situation in Czechoslovakia before 1948 then could be understood as a particularly radical variation of democratic socialism. This did not set us apart from the rest of Europe at that time in any way. I think if it hadn't been for the attempt in February 1948 to introduce a Soviet—that is, a completely Stalinist—system, we would have had a historic opportunity to start building a more radical variation on the welfare state than later developed in Europe from Sweden to Austria.

There was no anti-Russian or anti-Soviet tradition in Czechoslovakia. Our negative historical experience had been exclusively with the Germans, including the Austrians, and not with Russia, unlike the experience of Poland, for example. In 1945 the Soviet army was greeted almost everywhere among us as an army of liberation. And because at

Munich in 1938 our allies at the time, Britain and France, had betrayed us and sold us out to Hitler, popular sympathies after the war were on the side of the USSR, which stood out as our chief ally in the world.

The period of Stalinist political terror in our country was relatively short. Although Stalinism began to develop as early as 1948, its full development lasted only from 1949 to 1953, when Stalin died, and after that the brakes were put on the process of Stalinization. I think that it was for all these reasons that there were no upheavals in our country in 1956 like those in Poland and Hungary, not to mention East Germany. After this came a lengthy period, twelve years, during which though outwardly it was not noticeable, there was inwardly an even more profound and serious reform tendency developing within the CPC. For my own part I can say that as a Communist I definitely did not feel then that I was a member of some narrow sect condemned by the people. In 1968 I felt that my desire to understand and remake socialism along the lines that I have discussed was accepted by the people with a spirit of understanding. And so, in sum, the optimism of the reform Communists of 1968 was not just some naïve illusion; rather, the internal conditions in our country gave it firm ground to a considerable extent.

The Goal Was to Revitalize Socialism in General

Z.M.   However, somewhere in all this there began to arise a kind of dangerous tangle of logical contradictions, at first in my private thinking, then later in my political activity. I cannot and do not wish to speak for anyone else, but I think that I was not alone in this, that many reform Communists found themselves caught in similar contradictions.

Of course I never thought that uniform conditions existed in all of the socialist countries or that it was possible that the experience in our country could be simply transferred to the USSR or to Romania. You and I talked about this when we met in Stavropol in the spring of 1967.

M.G.   Yes, I remember. After hearing your basic ideas about possible democratization and a different way of managing the economy, I said that it was interesting and that I agreed that in your country all that might be possible, but in our country it simply could not be done.

z.m.   Yes, that is what you said then. So neither of us thought that conditions were the same in each country. But at the same time, in reflecting on the question of what "true socialism" was, I was thinking about this in the abstract, as had the classical authors of our movement, Marx and Engels, and Lenin in part as well. I was preoccupied with thoughts having to do with the models of relations in economic, social, and political fields that would not be capitalist, that is, would not turn our society back to the old prerevolutionary situation, but that would assure us at the same time that Stalinism would be overcome.

My concept that introduction of reform in Czechoslovakia would be merely one link in a chain of necessary general developments for socialism as a whole meant that I was not a proponent of some kind of narrow "national communism," that is, some separate path that would lead to a break with the USSR or with the entire so-called so-cialist camp—and I think many other Communists in our country then shared my views.

m.g.   But that is exactly what you were accused of. That you wanted to destroy the Warsaw Pact, the Council of Mutual Economic Assis-tance, international cooperation among socialist countries, and so forth.

z.m.   Yes, but that was one of the most lying accusations. In retro-spect I must say that it's a shame that it never even occurred to us that we might be charged with that, and therefore we were not pre-pared in practice for that accusation. There were also a number of reasons for that. Aside from anything else, the fact is that in 1968 approximately half of the party leadership would have considered any discussion about a possible break with the USSR as antisocialist. So before there could have been a break with the Soviet Union there would have been a split within the leadership of the CPC, and the Prague Spring would have been ended that way instead of the way it actually was.

But let us leave aside these political and practical reasons, along with the military and economic reasons. What I want to emphasize is the very way of thinking of the reform Communists at that time in our country. The fact is that precisely because of their loyalty to the ideals of socialism as a universal supranational value, because of their concepts that reform would serve to bring about gradual change in the entire socialist commonwealth, because otherwise it would not have been possible to revitalize socialism in one small country by itself—because of all that, the reform Communists proved to be totally disarmed in relation to the actual reality then in the surrounding countries. After the ouster of Khrushchev the leadership in all those countries wanted to put an end to any "dangerous experiments." We on the other hand wanted to be allowed to carry out an experiment that from their point of view would have been the most dangerous of all.

The Crushing of the Prague Spring—What it Meant

Z.M.   As far as the evolution of my own thinking goes—specifically my conception of socialism—all this that I have talked about, taken together, helped me after 1968 to gradually overcome the existing limitations.

The price paid for that, however, was terrible. Moreover, it was not I alone who paid it, and it was not only the reform Communists who paid it, but our entire people had to pay that price. With the result that later, after 1989, a settling of accounts took place in the form of rejection of any attempt whatsoever to reform socialism; instead, the restoration of capitalism began. And there was a certain logic to that.

Only after the defeat in 1968—and this became final later on when I spent a long time living in the West—only then did I part company with the idea of identifying socialism and its long-term historical prospects with the development of systems of the Soviet type. I myself came to understand—and by analysis of this subject I hope to help others understand—that political power of a totalitarian kind was a universal feature in those systems. All other aspects were conditioned by specific historical circumstances—from Russian and Chinese all the way to Czech and Hungarian. Although these systems were noncapitalist, not everything noncapitalist simply becomes socialist for that reason. And the opposite is also true: socialist elements can develop on the basis of a capitalist economy both in terms of people's value orientations and in institutional forms, for example, the welfare state.

M.G.   The events of August 1968 had serious consequences not only for the socialist countries and the world Communist movement, but for the world as a whole. As I have already said, it also had consequences in my own internal development and my understanding of what exactly was going on in our country. You are right that the consequences were severe. They were especially severe in Czechoslovakia, where people lost faith in the possibility of reform. But not only that. The suppression of the Prague Spring, which was an attempt to arrive at a new understanding of socialism, also engendered a very harsh reaction in the Soviet Union, leading to a frontal assault against all forms of free-thinking. The powerful ideological and political apparatus of the state acted decisively and uncompromisingly. This had an affect on all domestic and foreign policy and the entire development of Soviet society, which entered a stage of profound stagnation. It would seem that all this was enough for me to draw fundamental conclusions and reconsider my views. But to deny the idea that the Soviet system was identical with socialism, to deny that it embodied the advantages of socialism, I reached that point only after 1983, and not all at once even then. At first I made one more attempt at reforming the system, betting on the idea that by combining socialism with the scientific and technological revolution, using the advantages we believed were inherent in the planned economy, and making use of the concentration of governmental power, and so forth, things could be changed—that was the original plan. Our calculations were not confirmed in practice.

Z.M.   When we talk about the consequences of the defeat of the Prague Spring for the conception of socialism the main result remains disillusionment. Disbelief in the possibility of reforming a system of the Soviet type along democratic lines and at the initiative of the Communist parties that were in power began to spread and intensify. This continued up until the 1980s and the death of Brezhnev. The situation began to change little by little and by varying degrees only with the coming of your perestroika.

2. MORE DEMOCRACY, MORE SOCIALISM

The People Support Socialism Against the Nomenklatura

z.m.   When we met once again in December 1989 after a 22-year interval you said to me, among other things: "I don't know of course what we will succeed in doing, what my attempts at perestroika will end up with. But it is quite clear that for the time being the people will have the possibility of demonstrating their will; the state of affairs could not be worse than it was when I became head of the party."

From this it was clear to me that you were firmly convinced that the people would support socialism, not reject it. That the people could sort out those elements of Soviet reality which needed to be completely discarded and those which could be improved and revitalized. Unquestionably, your starting point then was that the purpose of perestroika was to reinvigorate socialism and make it viable, not to return to capitalism. Of course I agreed with that. But it seemed to me then that the slogan "more democracy" was not only decisive for you but also in a certain sense was in and of itself a sufficient condition for achieving that goal.

m.g.   Yes, in principle that was so. As we've already discussed, it was around 1983 that I concluded that Lenin had seen that his efforts had failed, that democracy for the mass of the people had in practice been stifled. And so for me the primary slogan to put forward in 1985 was "more democracy, more socialism." More democracy and more freedom in all things, both in economics and politics.

z.m.   But in reality at first, approximately until 1987, nothing much happened in regard to the advancement of democracy. "Acceleration" of the economy was discussed, but nothing about the need for democracy.

m.g.   Here you are criticizing me in the same way as our left radicals at that time, as though all you have to do is say the right word today and tomorrow it will become a reality.

z.m.   No, Misha, the radicals have always accused me of centrism, just as they have you. But I would like our conversation to take up the question of how you concretely understood the interrelationship of democracy and socialism in your political practice beginning in 1985.

m.g.   At the very beginning the question was one of relieving social and economic tensions. In order to do this it was necessary to set a different pace for economic development. We had lost momentum, had slipped down to zero growth, and essentially were not in any position to propose a program for the future. We had first of all to accelerate scientific and technological progress, but that presupposed democratization in the economic sphere, managerial autonomy for individual enterprises, placing them on a self-financing basis (without government subsidies), making them profitable, and so forth. I thought that was the essence of the problem.

So then, at first the task of political reform did not arise. Let me repeat that at first we set ourselves the task of assuring a decent life and social security for the people. It was not for the sake of formalities that all this was begun but for the sake of living human beings. There was a commonly held opinion: the shortest path to improving people's lives was through accelerating the pace of economic development, raising the productivity of labor, strengthening incentives to labor, all of which would simultaneously strengthen socialism. Society accepted and supported these aims. But a significant part of the *nomenklatura* in the party and the administrative structure responded apprehensively.

They saw a threat to their position and to their power in these reforms. By the end of 1987 the decisions of the January Central Committee plenum that year on personnel replacement policies had essentially been blocked, as had the decisions of the June plenum for radical economic reform, and within the new leadership of the country we came to the conclusion that the same fate that had befallen Khrushchev awaited us if the efforts made from above were not reinforced by support from below. Political reform was placed on the order of the day.

z.m.   So then, you—or, it would be better said in this case, you and your political allies in general—hoped that the people would come out against the *nomenklatura*, but at the same time would support and improve socialism in the sense of the basic principles of the Soviet system without "Stalinist deformations." Here in fact under new conditions the old belief shows itself that new personnel who would replace the existing bureaucracy could decide everything. I know that I am oversimplifying things greatly here, but in principle what happened was something like that, isn't it so?

m.g.   We proclaimed that we would give all officials a chance to reshape and redefine themselves, make their own choice, and in accordance with the position adopted we would conduct our policy of personnel changes. For many people a time had come that they had been waiting for all their lives. This part of the bureaucracy joined in the support of the reforms. But a large number of cadres took a wait-and-see attitude. They did not accept the new approach to things, especially that connected with democratization of the economy, the party, the Soviet system, and glasnost. Out of this refusal to accept new approaches came opposition to the reforms. It was clear to me that moving forward toward a new society would be difficult, that it was necessary to move gradually by evolutionary means, although in that case too it would not be possible to avoid opposition from the *nomenklatura*.

z.m.   All right, but you yourself were part of the *nomenklatura*, the head of it even, weren't you? So then, a certain part of the *nomenklatura* evidently had a different approach.

m.g.   Yes, that's correct. And I've spoken about this. But the main part of the *nomenklatura* didn't accept perestroika. I saw political reform as a way of solving two problems at once. First, to provide citizens with real control over the processes under way, to strengthen their rights and freedoms, and second, to solve the problem of official cadres through democratic forms, changing the role of the party and reviving the Soviets.

z.m.   Excuse me, Misha. All that is true enough. You have spoken about that many times, and everyone who wished for the success of your policies recognizes that. And it is absolutely undeniable that the *nomenklatura* was an important and perhaps a fatal danger for democracy. But because of this we cannot fail to pay attention to other dangers as well. Dangers which, as was shown in practice, became ultimately the most important threat to the development of democracy in the former Soviet Union. Namely, the fact that in Soviet society the only administrative and managerial structures that actually existed were those of the Stalinist type, that is, a monopoly of power held by the ruling party and by the bureaucratic-administrative apparatuses in all spheres of life. When emancipation comes to a society like that a dangerously chaotic situation arises that is absolutely inimical to democracy. After all, it is possible to emancipate only the society that has actually existed up until then. In that sense Brezhnev was unfortunately right that only his version of the Soviet—primarily Stalinist—system actually existed. And to try to emancipate a society like that simply by introducing elections and so forth could not result in the introduction of democracy or serve as a sufficient basis for the development of democracy. Rather, it merely marked the beginning of the disintegration of an effective mechanism of administration in general. How do you look at it today? Didn't an underestimation of that danger occur back then, beginning in 1987?

M.G. No, Zdeněk, even now when we know what direction the
changes took I consider, as I considered then, that the idea of socialism
can be put into practice only by expanding democratic processes, free
public discussion (glasnost), and political reforms in general. What I
hear in your comments are echoes of a rather widespread conception
that Russia had never grown up to the level of democracy and that
reforms should have been carried out somehow differently. I can agree
with you when you argue that Soviet society was an extremely difficult
and complex object for reform. In that you are correct. I was of the
same opinion from the very beginning of the reforms, and that is the
explanation for my choice in favor of evolutionary changes, my feeling
that cavalry charges were unacceptable. The reason for the failure of
the reforms is not that we took the path of democratic change. The
reasons lay elsewhere, in the vindictiveness of the reactionary forces
and the excessive revolutionism of the radicals. It is true that there was
not always sufficient logic in our actions, but as far as the basic choice
is concerned, in my opinion, there simply was no other way. You can
object that in China they are taking a different path. But I do think
that the reforms in China are being carried out taking the specific conditions of the country into account. Only the future will show to what
extent they prove effective.

z.M. I agree with you on that. I don't think China has found a solution that could have served as a model for you back then. Besides I
am no advocate of empty talk about what could have been "if only."
In general, that kind of thing is not of much significance. When there
were arguments about your policies I frequently defended your point
of view, that you could not have done anything differently if you did
not want to use force on a massive scale. And I see it as being to your
credit that you did not do that.

M.G. Yes, but I would like to emphasize one thing in this connection.
Placing our reliance on change by evolutionary means was precisely
testimony to our understanding of the complex character of our society
and of our desire not to let chaos take over in the process of reforming

it. And in the overall analysis this approach was justified and rendered the victory of the attempted coup of August 1991 impossible. The increased chaos and instability did not call into question the basic democratic choice.

Democracy Is Impossible Without Democratic Structures

z.m.   I agree, Misha. That very point affirms something very important. Democracy will not suddenly arise in a society in which it has not existed for decades simply because certain prohibitions have been removed, that all at once what was forbidden is now permitted. Destructive forces of any kind can misuse such a situation to their own advantage, because even when there are elections, very often it is the greatest demagogue who wins the most support. When there is no actually functioning structure that would make equilibrium possible, society itself can easily go off the rails and destruction can gain the upper hand instead of the emergence of new democratic structures.

I had my own experience along those lines in 1968 in Czechoslovakia: On the one hand, without freedom of expression the liberated atmosphere of the Prague Spring could not have arisen. On the other hand, the press often had a greater influence on the development of the situation than decisions by the political leadership, the party, the government, or parliament. And this was usually in a direction of hastiness and radicalism, as opposed to gradual evolutionary development. So then, I think I can imagine fairly vividly the difficulties that glasnost brought with it in your country.

m.g.   As I recall, from the end of 1987 on there was practically never a single session of the Politburo without debate over glasnost.

z.m.   I could say literally the same thing about meetings of the Politburo in Prague beginning in June 1968. Then in August Brezhnev joined the debate with his tanks and put an end to the discussion. But I would like to tell you quite frankly that in a certain sense, in my opinion, this simplified the situation for our reformers. We never had

to carry our practice through to a final test. It was never shown definitively what might or might not have been accomplished by the political
leaders of the Prague Spring. The tanks turned the Prague Spring into
a legend, but legends don't have to justify themselves with answers to
questions about what would have happened if they hadn't been legends.

I am speaking about this at such length so that it will be clear that
I absolutely do not wish to overestimate the ideas we had then, to
present them as some sort of recipe that could have changed everything, for example, if such a recipe had been used in Moscow in 1987.
But having made all these reservations, I will take the liberty of saying
that taking a society through a transition from a totalitarian system of
the Soviet type to democracy requires that structures be established in
a timely fashion and on the basis of well-thought-out principles, that
is, new political relations, new institutions, legal standards, and so
forth.

In 1968 in Czechoslovakia we tried to create such structures in par-
allel with the expansion of freedom. We did not have time to accomplish much, and almost the entire program of institutional reforms
remained solely on paper.

M.G.   The initial stage of perestroika was linked with an attempt to
make use of the existing structures, with all bets placed on a renewal
of personnel, but by the end of 1987, as I've already said, we came to
the conclusion that we couldn't get by without political reform. The
first free elections opened the road to power for new people. Thanks
to them we brought a critically thinking part of society into the realm
of government authority. An independent parliament set to work,
shouldering the burden of decisions regarding perestroika. Although
with difficulty, the structure of the government did begin to change,
and the dismantling of the old machinery of state got under way. And
by the way, new social organizations began to spring up like mush-
rooms after warm rain. Of course, the whole society was full of tur-
bulence and we were all being shaken about, but we held firm in regard
to the main line of development. The new supreme bodies of

government that began to function provided a certain guarantee of this. The new laws that were adopted opened the way for democracy, the market, new forms of property, and so forth. But that was the very thing that posed a threat to the old *nomenklatura*. No one excluded the *nomenklatura* from participating in the reforms, but the kind of choice it finally made—that is another question.

The Nomenklatura *Against Democracy*

Z.M.   So then, in practice, the question of whether the direction of democracy was toward the renewal and strengthening of socialism— that question took a back seat under the pressure of necessity, the need to fight for real influence over the government against the aggressive conservative majority of *nomenklatura* officials.

M.G.   Why do you say that? Through our political reforms we gave a powerful forward impulse to the development of democracy. Through the elections, glasnost, and the new parliament we strength- ened society's control over the changes taking place, and over the *no- menklatura* as well, and for this very reason it's impossible to portray the perestroika process in black-and-white terms: that would be a great oversimplification.

The democratization of society opened the doors wide for fresh forces to flow into all the structures of power. Even part of the old *nomenklatura*—some earlier, others later—made their choice in favor of the policies of perestroika. But it is also true that many of them simply did not accept the reforms, especially among the party bureau- cracy: they turned out to be unwilling to work under democratic con- ditions and therefore tried in every possible way to oppose the expan- sion and consolidation of democracy. In order to hold onto their positions, some of the *nomenklatura* went so far as to make an alliance with nationalist forces. What was called the "war of sovereignties," beginning in 1990, was at the same time a process supported by party apparatchiks in the republics and in local areas (once again not all, but a considerable portion) in the hope that, once they were free from control by the center, or at least with that control weakened, they could fortify their own positions.

Z.M.   So then, the *nomenklatura*, precisely in order to get away from reform policies, had an interest in dissolving the USSR. Getting away from Gorbachev presupposed dissolving the union as a kind of pedestal on which he stood as president of the USSR. Consequently, one may say along these lines that what came to be called the August 1991 coup was actually in preparation for a long time before that.

M.G.   No, I think that conclusion would be wrong. The perestroika process was unfolding in too contradictory a way, and events could have followed one scenario or another or possibly even a third.

At first the antireform forces wanted to achieve their goals by freeing themselves from control by the reformers in the center. For this purpose they might make use of what we could call entirely democratic procedures, demanding my resignation and expressing lack of confidence in me at the Congress of People's Deputies and at plenary sessions of the party Central Committee. The plans of the conservative forces included a minimum program: to break the will of the president and general secretary, to force him to change his political positions and come over to their side. On the republic and oblast level the elite played its game by trying to strengthen its own position as against the center. Therefore, one cannot say that a deliberate intention to dissolve the Soviet Union was part of the plans of the *nomenklatura* in order to save their own positions. After all, it was evident that the downfall of the central union government would affect the interests of the *nomenklatura* itself fundamentally, and not just on the unionwide level. You could put it this way: a different central government would have been to its liking, but not the elimination of that government altogether. The August coup was not a logical consequence of the reforms.

And the fact that the coup was defeated is a confirmation of what I've just said. The tragedy was that in effect it sharply intensified the disintegration processes in the USSR and opened the door for radical extremist forces.

Z.M.   So then, you think that if the new Union Treaty had been successfully concluded, the possibility of evolutionary development would have remained, including the socialist orientation?

M.G.   Yes, without a doubt. But with the understanding that we had already arrived at a new conception of socialism.

3. FREEDOM OF CHOICE EITHER EXISTS OR IT DOESN'T

Z.M.   One of the basic demands, Misha, that you linked with your policy of perestroika, especially after 1987, was the demand for freedom of choice. To give the people the possibility of freely choosing what path they wish to follow and what policy they wish to support. However, this is always a very complex and contradictory thing, not only in a transition from a totalitarian system to democracy. On top of that, when changing the system is involved, it is also a very risky business, because if freedom of choice is taken seriously, one cannot know with full certainty in advance what people are actually going to choose. As you showed in practice, you really did take this demand seriously. And that was true both in relation to the possibility of choice in the countries of the Soviet bloc, where you rejected the traditional policy of intervention, supervision, and the use of force, and in relation to the development of Soviet society, where you also refused to use force to put your concepts of perestroika into effect. To this day some people blame you for this and others praise you. What did you think people in the USSR and throughout the Soviet bloc would choose if they had the real possibility of free choice? Wasn't this an oversimplified approach on the part of the reformers?

Freedom is always of value in and of itself, but certain conditions are necessary in order for it to make sense in people's lives. Thus, freedom of the press, let's say, has real significance only when people can read; in a society of illiteracy freedom of the press is irrelevant. Freedom of choice in a situation where people do not have sufficient information about the possible alternatives they can choose from suf-

fers in a somewhat similar way. It leads most often to a rejection of
that which people experienced as bad. As far as the future goes, people
choose their own concepts, which are often illusions, rather than a
realistic alternative, because they actually don't know about it. Only
over the course of time, as people acquire their own experience under
conditions of freedom, can that change. I think this is exactly the situation that prevails now in the society that previously was called "actually existing socialism."

What Was Meant by the "Socialist Choice"

M.G.   To begin with, I want to disagree with you. You were talking
about how difficult it is to make use of a newly acquired freedom,
especially when society and its citizens have lived for many years
under a totalitarian system. Often this results in outright rejection,
because people have not been prepared for something different and
they don't know how to use the freedom that has been achieved. I
will say frankly that however logical this line of reasoning is, there is
an academic flavor to it (and by this I do not mean to express con-
tempt for theory!). I passed through various stages in my own experience: exploring, developing a new conception, formulating a policy
corresponding to that conception, and putting these plans into effect—then there were the reforms themselves, new discoveries, and
conclusions during the course of perestroika. This experience leads
me to the conclusion that people can make use of freedom by taking
the road of reform, of gradual evolutionary development. On the
other hand, a choice in favor of revolutionary extremism leads to
chaos, destruction, and often to a new lack of freedom. This is exactly
what follows from our experience.

We did not take the option of the use of force to impose certain
artificial models invented in someone's office. Our choice was to hu-
manize and reorganize the country through democratization and evolutionary reforms within the framework of a socialist choice. Today I
am even more convinced of this choice, because the attempt in recent

years to impose a far-reaching return to capitalism, and the forcible introduction of capitalist reforms, has ended in failure and has been rejected by a majority of the people.

Complaints can be brought against the reformers of the perestroika era in connection with one or another miscalculation in practical work. But the service they rendered, and this is the most essential thing for an evaluation of what they accomplished, was that they began these reforms and sought to carry them through democratically, moving forward step by step within the framework of the choice that had been made, expanding the boundaries of freedom, and constantly increasing the depth and scale of the changes.

And now let me also give an answer to your question: What did I think the choice of people in the USSR and Soviet bloc would be when they received a real opportunity to make a free choice?

My view on this was unambiguous—people would make a choice in favor of democracy and in the framework of a democratic process. Using mechanisms of free choice, and new democratic institutions, they would decide what kind of society corresponded to their interests. From the very beginning it was clear to me that this would be a long drawn-out path with many difficulties; surprising turns of events, and new discoveries and losses, were not excluded. And actually that is what happened. The people of our countries are seeking the optimal variant. For some this process is going on less painfully, but in the post-Soviet space it is proceeding in a highly dramatic way.

However, the process of evolutionary reforms, as I've said, was cut short, and events have followed a different scenario. Still, the game is not over. In the last analysis everything will be determined by whether the citizens of Russia and of the other countries of the Commonwealth of Independent States retain a genuine possibility of free choice. If so, then in these countries also we can expect new and very substantial changes of direction in the development of the reforms.

z.m.   Yes, I agree that freedom of choice is not a one-time action, but rather a prolonged process of searching. And I am willing to agree with your arguments in favor of evolutionary reforms within whose framework there is created a guarantee for the successful realization by the people of the right to make a free choice. People should have the right to choose, but that means not only that no one forbids them from choosing but also that they actually make a choice between alternatives. But such a thing is possible only under conditions of democracy with extensive information about possible alternatives and genuinely free elections.

Yet when you and I met in 1989, we evaluated the development of the situation in the countries of "actually existing socialism" somewhat differently, including in regard to the long-term prospects of socialism.

M.G.   Yes, but this is natural, because we were dealing with one particular reality and the trends that had appeared at that time, but later events of a different kind occurred, which drastically changed the picture, especially in our countries. The course of the reforms and their direction changed drastically. But you'll agree, I'm sure, that this entire process is still in its initial stage and people once again are facing a choice. What choice they will make depends again on whether the conditions for a free democratic choice are preserved. Today the defense of democracy, glasnost, human rights, and civil liberties are of paramount importance.

This last observation has special significance for Russia, where the crisis has reached a point of unparalleled acuteness and under the impact of this crisis various defenders of democracy, that is, people who defended democracy in the recent past, are now calling for the president to assume the role of a "Russian Pinochet."

I can confirm that there is a desire for consolidation of democratic forces. In Russia today there are many discussions about the prospects for Social Democracy and the role of the socialist idea in building a new democratic society. The interest in intellectual circles is so great that some individuals who at one time were famous for their liberalism are now declaring their adherence to Social Democracy.

You know, Zdeněk, that the process of profound reevaluation and critical reflection began in my case after my report on the seventieth anniversary of the October revolution, and I publicly expressed my thoughts in this regard in fully worked-out form at the Central Committee Plenum of February 1988 and the Party Conference of June 1988. In 1989, after the elections, when we saw what attitude the people really had toward the CPSU and the *nomenklatura*, what it really thought, and what its attitude was toward democracy and glasnost, there began a period of accumulation of experience that brought us to the conclusion that it was necessary to arrive at a new conception of socialism. Since that time I have been occupied more and more with the question: What are the criteria for calling something socialist? It seemed to me that the main one had to do with: What is the position of the individual in society? From that moment on, you might say, the road I have taken has essentially been the Social Democratic conception of socialism.

z.m.   Those who have followed your speeches from afar have noticed that instead of socialism you more and more often have begun to speak about "the idea of socialism" and the "socialist choice." It was clear that you were trying to distinguish the existing Soviet totalitarian system from the concept of socialism. However, a "socialist choice" had been made, according to the conception of socialism at the time of the October 1917 revolution, and that choice was made, under revolutionary conditions, by your grandfather and of course by the grandfathers and even great grandfathers of those generations which faced a new choice in 1987. When these generations had the real possibility of a free choice, they of course had to proceed, not on the basis of their great grandfathers and grandfathers' experiences, but on their own. The experience of life under "actually existing socialism" was for the most part unsatisfactory, and there was no experience whatsoever with capitalism, with life under that system, whether it be in the West or in the so-called Third World. Consequently, the odds were not favorable for the rational reformist policies of "centrists," but the situation was ideal for demagogues of the radical left and right. This situation can be briefly stated in one sentence:

Everyone Knew What They Did Not Want

Z.M.   But this is precisely a situation in which people would use freedom of choice simply to reject the existing state of affairs. What would
happen next—no one had any definite idea about that. The final result
of it all was simply total rejection of any concept of socialism whatsoever. I think it was exactly in this way, or something like it, that the
first steps were taken on the road that opened the possibility of free
choice in the countries of "actually existing socialism."

M.G.   I think it is still too early to draw any definitive conclusions. The
processes going on in Poland, in Hungary, in Bulgaria, and—not least
important—in Russia testify to this. The socialist idea has not yet had
its funeral. For its own part it has abandoned the claim to a monopoly.
And this is the road toward dialogue, mutual enrichment, and a new
role in the society of the future, the search for which has already begun.

Z.M.   More than that, we both reject the view that calls into question
the very possibility of using freedom of choice. Nevertheless, a question
remains: Was it possible—especially on the part of intellectuals educated in Marxism—to develop more specific ideas concerning socialist
alternatives?

M.G.   This is again one of the most complex questions, the role of the
intellectuals. I think that we will talk about this in more detail when we
discuss the critics of perestroika both on the left and on the right. For
now, let me make just one general observation. When our intellectuals
adopted the idea of perestroika they did a great deal to advance the
cause of perestroika in society. Without them our cause would not have
unfolded as it did. But it very quickly became apparent that even those
who began to advocate pluralism and to support new ideas were not
prepared for relatively fundamental change. Even those who before perestroika presented bold and unorthodox concepts in the social sciences
turned out to be incapable of implementing scientifically based proposals
for a transition to a qualitatively new state of society. That which ini-

tially seemed extremely courageous in the years of stagnation was usually just a critical analysis of the previous state of affairs, but there were no new constructive ideas. Many of our intellectuals continued to criticize and support not so much objective research as denial and rejection of everything in the past entirely and completely, as became the fashion. In the political sphere the conservatives of course made use of this, accusing the intellectuals of negativism and of "blackening Soviet reality."

z.m. I can only add my perspective, how I perceived the situation then from outside the Soviet Union. German television frequently broadcast interviews with passers-by on the streets of various Soviet cities. I remember one quite ordinary woman answering an interviewer's question as to what democracy meant to her. She answered quite simply: well-stocked shelves in the stores. Approximately at the same time prominent delegates at various congresses were saying that, after all, socialism existed in Canada and Switzerland. It sounded as though they were singing in unison with that woman in the street. In October 1988 the Spanish Socialists organized a symposium on perestroika in Barcelona, where a delegation from the USSR was present with many members. There were Soviet journalists and scholars from various fields. At that conference one economist who in general was quite an attractive figure (and why make a secret of it, it was Shmelyov) was asked which tendency the current policy of the CPSU was closest to, Social Democracy or Leninism. He answered: "We're sick and tired of all these isms! The main thing is that there should be sausage." This was not only very primitive but also disrespectful toward those who had gathered there: these were socialists, people of left-wing views who were not just interested in developments in the USSR but were actively supporting the new policies of perestroika.

m.g. How did you feel about it?

z.m. I just felt ashamed. Later I came over to Shmelyov and told him this, and he answered: "We're sick and tired of all these leftists!" I simply asked him how many leftists he had met in the West and who he had spoken with, and that's where our conversation ended. The point is that the behavior of some of your people could be taken advantage of not only by the conservatives in your country but also by the antisocialist right-wing forces in the West.

M.G.   What happened in this case was a foul-up. It was necessary not only to criticize but also to expose the misdeeds of Stalinism and Stalinist methods, but that shouldn't have meant pushing everything else into the background. Our scholars and scientists often preferred to make journalistic statements relating to the particular moment, anything to avoid being accused of conservatism. Hardly anyone really got involved in working out new policies as a way of helping the reforms.

Freedom of Choice Meant "Get Away From Moscow"

Z.M.   Never, even after the August 1968 Soviet intervention, did it enter my head that I could remain a socialist and at the same time turn my back on or express scorn for what was going on in the USSR. On the contrary, developments in your country were for me a fundamental factor which, as it then seemed, had buried the hopes for any good prospects for socialism in general. But later when a certain Gorbachev appeared at the head of the CPSU, my hopes revived. I will admit, however, that there was a large personal element in this: if I hadn't known you, perhaps I wouldn't have had great hopes. But I can imagine what your thinking was about many things. And because I had faith in you I also had faith in your hopes for socialism. Lastly, I made a public acknowledgement of this in my first article about you in L'Unità immediately after your rise to the head of the party at the beginning of April 1985.

So for me—and this is purely on a personal level—it's very important to find out directly from you what you thought about the general prospects for socialism when you decided not only not to intervene in developments in the Soviet bloc countries with military force but also not to exert effective political pressure on the leaders of those countries for the sake of your own policy of perestroika. What was the decisive

thing here: a desire to overcome the division of Europe into two separate blocs and to get out of the Cold War? Or a conviction that freedom
of choice is necessary for everyone, including the people in countries
belonging to the Soviet bloc?

For me in 1968 the situation was much simpler: we could not change
the situation, the division of Europe into two blocs, and therefore took
it as an underlying condition of our political conceptions. You on the
other hand had taken many specific steps toward overcoming the division of the world even before 1989, and your attitude toward the
development of the Soviet bloc must have been influenced by all that.

M.G.   The thing that was of decisive importance, Zdeněk, was our
arriving at the new thinking, the recognition of the interdependence
and wholeness of the world—with all its contradictions, a very complex but interrelated, which is to say a unified whole. But the recognition of the fact that despite all differences we are one civilization
posed the question of "a new world order" in a different way.

The movement toward a new world order does not mean a leveling
out or smoothing over of differences or the imposition of a single model
for everyone. Every people must have a real *right of free choice,* with
its history, its culture, its mentality, and its potential taken into account.
From this it follows that development must include *diversity in the
various paths of development.* Freedom of choice must not be restricted
for anyone, no matter what bloc their country belonged to; that is,
both Czechoslovakia and the Soviet Union must have it. Let everyone
enjoy the right to free choice.

And so there was both a desire to overcome the division of the world
into blocs and a recognition of freedom of choice regardless of what
kind of social system existed in a particular country. The West often
thought that this had nothing to do with them, that it was a matter
affecting only the socialist countries, while nothing in their countries
would have to change. But that was a mistake, for which they are
already beginning to pay.

This is where my "revisionism," if you will, Zdeněk, had its beginning. I proceeded from the assumption that the fate of socialism could

not be resolved without applying the principles of freedom of choice, pluralism, and democracy, to which all entities involved in world politics had a right, including within the socialist commonwealth. I had ceased to be a supporter of the idea that socialism was a special formation to which the general standards of civilization did not apply. But it is also true that I, like you, thought that the result of free choice in the socialist countries would be a synthesis of democracy and socialism. But that idea was not a precondition for, nor the starting point of, my position, although it was an accompanying aspect.

z.m.   In reality, however, the social and political systems of "actually existing socialism" turned out to be more stricken with decay and decomposition than we had supposed. But what you have just said means that the existence of the "socialist commonwealth" in your view was a socialist value only in the event that it was a community based on the freedom of choice of its people. But if the existing order in any one of those countries could not maintain itself, but simply collapsed as a result of the free choice of its people, this system which had called itself socialism, strictly speaking, was not socialism at all, because socialism without democracy and freedom of choice for the people is impossible. There is a certain logic to this point of view, of course, which is quite different from the reasoning of those who accuse you of "surrendering" the countries of the so-called socialist camp to the whims of fate.

m.g.   Yes, I'm familiar with such accusations. My answer is this: What did I surrender, and to whom? Poland to the Poles, the Czech lands to the Czechs, Hungary to the Hungarians, and so on. At the same time this was not something that just came along out of the blue only in 1989. Immediately after the funeral of my predecessor, Chernenko, I called a conference of political leaders of the Warsaw Pact countries and told them clearly that now we were actually going to do what we had for a long time been declaring: we would adhere strictly to the principle of equality and independence, which also included the responsibility of each party for the development of its own country.

This meant that we would not commit acts of intervention or interference in their internal affairs. My counterparts at that conference, as I came to understand later, did not take what I said seriously. But I did adhere to this principle and never departed from it.

What was of prime significance for me in all this was always the necessity for freedom of choice in each country, as we have already discussed. As for the revitalization of socialism, I also proceeded from the assumption that countries like Czechoslovakia and Hungary had stronger democratic traditions and that social and democratic changes would take place there more quickly.

z.m.   That's fine, Misha, but still there are some questions remaining in this area. After all, both Hungary and Czechoslovakia, as well as Poland, had quite an unambiguous experience—namely, that their own attempts at democratic reform had been suppressed by force. In the first two countries by direct Soviet military intervention, and in Poland by their own military and police forces, which, however, could afford to do this only because of support from Moscow. You personally of course did not bear responsibility for this, but it was part of the legacy left to you by the former rulers of the Kremlin.

The forcible suppression of democratic forces in those countries left painful wounds, and it could be said that not only society, but the Communist parties as well, had been maimed by those actions. This was most distinctly expressed in Czechoslovakia, where for twenty years, with virtually no change in its composition, a leadership sat in power after being elevated to that position literally by Soviet tanks. In such a situation to say: "You are now free; we will no longer interfere in your affairs"—that is like telling a person whose legs have been broken: "Well, come on now, you can go where you want."

m.g.   The issue was not presented in this way, Zdeněk. On the one hand we had a very definite orientation, which meant, for example, an end to the doctrine of "limited sovereignty." We renounced that doctrine. But it cannot be said that we were indifferent to the fate of these countries. We sought to give support to reform forces there, to support them not only politically but also by substantial economic aid, for example, in Poland; we supported Mladenov in Bulgaria and reformers in Hungary.

z.m.   All right, but excuse me, I still can't let the question of Czechoslovakia pass by in silence. Beginning in 1985 I naturally followed Soviet policy in relation to Prague very closely. And I can say to you, taking full responsibility for my words, that I understood it as de facto support for the leadership and the line that directly descended from the suppression of the Prague Spring.

m.g.   But we did not support them . . .

z.m.   Excuse me, Misha, but I have to interrupt you. In the spring of 1987 when you came to Prague our entire people expected that you would say, at the minimum, something like what you said later in Germany: "Life will punish those who act too late." We expected that in some way you would make it understood that you sympathized with the Prague Spring. After all those actually were your real sympathies. I'll go so far even to say that in Czechoslovakia then a large part of society linked great hopes with your policies, more than in any other socialist country at that time.

m.g.   I felt that when I traveled there. I was surprised, when meeting people out on the streets, to see signs with slogans like this: "Gorbachev stay here for at least a year." This made a strong impression on me.

z.m.   There, you see! But what you said to these people was that they should be proud of what they had achieved in the previous twenty years, that is, since 1968; that in 1968 there had been chaos, but the difficult times had now passed; that you had "been with them" during that difficult time! Yes, you had been with them, together with your tanks! How could you talk that way? I couldn't understand it then, and I still don't understand it—although I am willing to take into consideration any pressure on you from the conservatives on the Soviet Politburo at that time.

M.G.   Wait, Zdeněk, let's talk about this calmly. First, that was only the spring of 1987, and we were still only seeking our way, forming our conception. And if the direction was obvious, the orientation un-derstandable, the intention clear, then, our movement, our road toward that, required carefully weighed steps and thinking things through. At the same time I want to say that I did have a certain respect for Husák [the leader of the Czechoslovak Communist Party imposed after the Soviet invasion in 1968]. I considered then and consider to this day that he represented a variant on several possibilities, a somewhat re-alistic variant, given the situation in 1969. But I did not praise the intervention or the policies that ensued after the invasion. I simply wanted to say that in 1968 there had been a complex stage in history, that we especially supported what had existed at first, but later the situation had become more strained, and tragic events had occurred. My reasoning at that time was as follows: "Today I don't want to go back to that complicated and dramatic time in history. I only want to tell people that it was not in vain that you lived through the last twenty years. Your country has accomplished a great deal. Let us think and move along together; let's cooperate." I invited them, so to speak, to join in on perestroika.

Finally, don't forget, Zdeněk, my declaration as early as March 1985 that we were unambiguously renouncing the "Brezhnev doc-trine." Instead, there would be equality, independence, noninterference in one another's affairs, and total responsibility by the leadership of each country in the socialist commonwealth for the state of affairs in its own country.

Z.M.   Misha, I have no doubt of your good intentions, but what you said at the time had the reverse effect on people. You disillusioned them terribly. Your words sounded like you were placing your blessing on the past. You offered a challenge that people should follow the road of perestroika, but under the leadership of tried and true supporters of the policy of "normalization," who had shown themselves to be loyal flunkies of the Brezhnev era—which in your own country you condemned as the period of stagnation. It doesn't make any sense to take this now as a reproach against you. I only want to explain what effect it had on me. And to ask quite candidly: Didn't you really know that without a condemnation of the intervention, and without political rehabilitation of the Prague Spring, it would be impossible to carry out your own policy of perestroika in Czechoslovakia!?

M.G.   Well, what is one to say here? The Politburo had a position on this question. It had been agreed to. I can add to that that as a preventive measure the Prague leadership wanted me to make a statement of open support for the events of late 1968 during my visit. But I didn't agree to that. Although you are right when you speak of a certain ambiguity in my statement. The explanation for that is that neither in my own country nor outside of it was I yet able to take the measures which I later took. A certain length of the road still had to be traveled before that could be done.

We sympathized with everyone who supported perestroika. But nowhere did we try to give a push from the outside to the internal processes: that would have been a return to the old practices. Toward the end of his effective functioning Husak came to Moscow, we had a lot of talks, and he wanted to be assured of direct support on questions of personnel. My answer contained an expression of confidence that they themselves would resolve these problems in such a way as to contribute to further change.

The situation was of course a contradictory one for us, and this had to do not only with Czechoslovakia. I traveled to Cuba, and there the entire Cuban leadership with Fidel at its head was sitting in front of me. I saw that the situation was a tense one, that at any moment an explosion could occur. But after my speech, and the words I spoke about decades of cooperation, and our desire to maintain and continue that, the circumstances of the meeting changed. And I said approximately the following: what we are doing now is necessary for us. But that does not mean you have to do the same thing. You are in a completely different country, and a different situation. Our attitude is one of confidence in what you do. That is obviously necessary for you. It is your choice, and no questions about it arise on our part. In a word, we are not the center and we do not issue orders. We are willing to share our experience, and we have done so. We can explain and present the arguments as to why we have done what we have done, but in no way are we trying to impose this.

z.m.   Yes, I understand. But let's go back to the original question. It follows that you did not ask yourself the question: What would happen to socialism in the countries where the *nomenklatura* was sitting in the leadership posts, a *nomenklatura* that was worse than the one in the USSR? Regardless of that fact, you allowed them to do what they wanted, and left them in the leading positions.

m.g.   Listen to the way you're arguing: "left them in the leading positions."

z.m.   Well, all right, I accept your comment. But the fact remains that these people were sitting there and waiting for the comrade to be so good as to issue an order. It's true that you didn't issue orders. But at the same time there persisted that terrible legacy that had been left to you after Brezhnev, and consequently you did have an obligation and a responsibility to actively do something about it.

m.g.   Nevertheless, Zdeněk, your arguments—how can I tell you this?—remain in the channel of the old approach of which you yourself became a victim. We were living in a different time, operating under a different system of coordinates, and we could not just issue orders. Still, perestroika was functioning, and it operated with an effect, as it turned out, much stronger than the so-called "hand of Moscow." And we withstood a very difficult experience—not engaging in intervention. I think that we established a unique precedent in this way, one whose significance has not yet been appreciated as it deserves to be.

Z.M.   In conclusion, one more point. One of the results of free choice
in the Warsaw Pact countries was a development in the direction of
"let's get away from Moscow." At the same time this was the decisive
impulse behind the disintegration, and ultimately the collapse of the
USSR itself. Hence, it was far from being only a matter of the fate of
the so-called "socialist choice." But those are the consequences of
freedom.

The Process of Choosing Is Not Yet Finished

M.G.   I don't think that your analysis can be considered correct in
this case. The processes taking place in the Warsaw Pact countries were
by no means the determining factor in the disintegration of the USSR.
Possibly their example played some role, but the main causes of the
collapse of the USSR are to be found in what was actually going on in
the Soviet Union, which you and I have discussed. Moreover, developments in the former republics of the USSR cannot be considered
completed. It is only now becoming clear what complex problems they
are confronted with. We cannot consider the present phase of developments as already fully known to us—what new things have been
opened up as a result of free choice and on what scale. Within the
framework of democracy and free choice very little has yet been decided, and everything still remains before us. As we've already said,
freedom of choice is not a one-time action; it is a process of exploration
under conditions of freedom.

Z.M.   It seems to me that a positive result of what has happened up
until now is the fact that the concept of the "socialist world" as a
special and separate formation has disappeared, that is, of a world
existing in only certain countries. Socialism is beginning to be understood as one of a large number of forces operating in the worldwide
process of a search for further ways for modern civilization to develop.
But I would like to talk about that as a separate question.

        To put it briefly, the main thing is that a path for further develop-
ment was opened. I will not presume to predict when and where it will

lead, but the possibility for exploration is there, including exploration consistent with socialist values and concepts.

M.G.   Yes, I also think that the main thing is that we have opened a path in order to proceed farther. We did what had to be done: we gave freedom, glasnost, and political pluralism; we gave democracy. We broke apart, dismantled, and destroyed the totalitarian regime and freed the individual. Another service we performed was that we did not construct models or try to force society to fit into such models. People have the possibility of free choice, and there are wide open spaces for pluralistic democracy, political liberty, and freedom of thought. I think that, within the framework of the current of opinion that includes the democratic conception of socialism, we conducted ourselves as people committed to socialist values.

Z.M.   Although what you have just said is, strictly speaking, a confession of liberalism.

M.G.   I'd like it to be defined more precisely what is meant by a confession of liberalism.

Z.M.   I think, just as you do, that liberalism does not contradict socialism, although in and of itself it is insufficient.

M.G.   Let us continue the discussion on that topic later.

4. AN AIRPLANE TOOK OFF, NOT KNOWING
WHERE IT WOULD LAND

Z.M.   The comparison of the policies of perestroika with a helpless airplane that has taken off but doesn't know where it's going to land began to be used frequently, especially after 1989, by those who criticized the new policy above all because they were afraid to change the existing system (or in general did not want to). In a definite sense, it was mainly the slogan of the conservatives. At the same time, it embodied a certain element of truth: the end result of historical processes that involve fundamental change always remains open and unclear; no one can say with full certainty, "We will end up here." Thus, the airplane image can also be used by those supporters of perestroika who have a critical attitude—for example, those critical of the desire to carry out change with the haste that rules out carefully considered action and weakens the determining influence of the political leadership. These critics, just like you, were opposed to the radicals of that time. How did you yourself perceive the airplane analogy?

M.G.   The writer Yuri Bondarev first used this analogy at the Nineteenth Party Conference. It aroused a feeling of protest in me, but I did not openly show my feeling at the time. The delegates who spoke from the democratic point of view evaluated Bondarev's words as an attempt to discredit the policies of perestroika. The writer in fact condemned the reformers for having dared to take a new road that in many respects was unexplored. This was of course a rejection of the reforms.

I now recall a Soviet film that appeared before perestroika. It was entitled *The Crew* and told about a dramatic situation faced by the crew of a Soviet airliner that made international flights. For us it was an extraordinary film, with such talented actors as Georgy Zhzhenov and Leonid Filatov. They found themselves in what seemed a hopeless situation. They were at an airport where everything was trembling because of an earthquake, and a huge fire had started—giant flames were leaping up. The commander of the airplane spoke some words whose inner meaning went beyond that particular situation: "It's not safe to fly, but we can't stay here. So we're going to fly." That's the way it was with our country and perestroika.

Still, Bondarev forced us to think many things over more carefully and to weigh them on the scales of politics. It became clear that perestroika had to be more energetically defended and, even more important, had to be explained more fully, including to its own supporters. Above all, we could not look at it as a process in which everything was clearly defined in advance, as though we knew what we would achieve and when. The main thing was to establish one idea firmly in people's minds: our movement forward in the framework of the policies of perestroika was not going to be simple and easy and free of problems. We had to absorb the lessons of Khrushchev's example. He tried to make the party program look more attractive and in the process fell into the mistake of replacing realistic strategy and tactics with prescriptions of a populist kind.

Political Centrism and "Dangerous Rocks Under Water"

Z.M.   It also seems to me that the difficulties arising in connection with the metaphor about the airplane were an expression of the profound contradictions in the policies of perestroika. The problem was that, although the metaphor was to a certain extent well founded, it would have been politically impossible to unite with those who proclaimed this metaphor as a slogan because that would have meant a suicidal unification with forces that rejected fundamental change of the system. You and your policies, while they sought gradual development and the forestalling of conflicts, had the ultimate goal of changing the system—a contradiction that would have been difficult to resolve. Speaking in an oversimplified way, one of the dangerous "underwater rocks" of political centrism was blatantly manifested here: one had to admit that the conservative critique of perestroika was more realistic on a number of questions than the enthusiasm of the progressives, but the proponents of that criticism could not be supported because that would discredit the position of the centrists (or moderates) in the eyes of society and would strengthen the hand of irresponsible radicalism.

M.G.   Yes, I agree with that, but at the same time I would like to say that for me there was something else that was important. The process of change of course posed constantly new questions that it was necessary to think about and seek answers for. But in this search we wanted to put an end to the old Bolshevik tradition of creating an ideological construct and then trying to force society to fit that mold without taking into account the resources and ultimately the opinions of the citizenry.

z.m.   However, it is precisely the carefully thought-out specific steps and practical politics that are often impossible during a time of fundamental and radical change. On the basis of my own personal experience in 1968 I can say that oversimplified views often win out instead. At that time it was typical for us that those who had the biggest influence on public opinion (first of all the press, radio, and television), instead of evaluating the various standpoints of the politicians in relation to the main problems by means of concrete analysis, simply divided politicians into three groups—progressives, dogmatists, and centrists. In so doing they often portrayed the latter as people who were more cowardly than responsible. Perhaps this is stated in too biased a way, because I myself was numbered among the centrists at that time, but I think that in principle that is how it was. Depending on what label you were given your political position was automatically either praised or rejected.

m.g.   It was the same with us. The old Communist habit of labeling people, of categorizing them "once and for all," reappeared under new conditions.

z.m.   And that did a great deal of harm to reform policies.

m.g.   Strictly speaking, this was Bolshevism turned inside out. And you are right, Zdeněk, when you say that it often made it impossible for us to give fairly resolute support to more realistic kinds of political measures and played into the hands of irresponsible radicalism. Often it divided people who held views fairly close to one another. Or on the other hand, under the pressure of this kind of situation, people who were quite different became allies.

z.m.   Ryzhkov in his 1992 book of memoirs about perestroika writes in a fairly detailed way that his main objection to perestroika was that more and more space was being given to hasty actions instead of those that were carefully thought out. This was mainly in the process of economic transformation, where unrealistic views such as the slogan of "reform in 500 days" ultimately began to gain prevalence. I must admit that, not only when I read Ryzhkov's book, but also when the "500 days" program began to be promoted, I considered it completely mistaken. But you and I discussed this openly at the time, and as I recall, you also had no confidence in the "500 days" miracle. But whoever wanted to open the road to further development then, and not to strengthen the influence of the dangerous forces (mainly officials of the *nomenklatura*) who had already begun to openly denounce perestroika, could not get into a conflict with supporters of the "500 days" program, and also could not in all respects agree with the views of their opponents.

That is an example of the "underwater rocks" encountered by the adherents of centrism. In my own experience in 1968 there was another "underwater rock" which I remember quite vividly to this day. The conservative critics in the party at the time held the view, which was by and large realistic, that eliminating censorship would make it possible, aside from anything else, for openly anti-Soviet views to be expressed, which would politically undermine the positions of the reformers and strengthen the proponents of intervention in Moscow. But it was impossible for the centrists to move in the direction of uniting with these critics, because the centrists valued freedom of speech and the press as one of the cornerstones of the reform policy, and they knew that if censorship was restored, people would cease to have confidence in the reformers.

M.G.   That's right, but it should also be added that the proponents of critical views always represented particular social strata and political tendencies. Realistic politics can never fail to take that into account. Lenin, in his day, opposed the expulsion of Kamenev and Zinoviev from the Central Committee because they represented a particular tendency whose existence would not cease after they were expelled. I personally cannot, for example, anathematize Ligachev. This was a man who in his own way was honorable, who openly presented his views and defended his position. True, in the final stages of our joint work he did some sneaky things after all, operating behind our backs, but that doesn't change the essence of the matter—he did reflect the interests of certain circles in society.

Society Knew of No Alternatives

z.m. Misha, it would probably be worth going back to a question we touched on earlier: Was it or was it not possible to have several alternative paths of development in perestroika? Until now we have discussed this only in connection with the fact that a large number of Soviet intellectuals limited their criticism to the Stalinist system and could neither propose any new conceptions for development in the future nor even call for discussion of that subject. But that by no means exhausts the problem. Experts can formulate alternatives only partially, only as an initial impetus. The essential thing is the extent to which society itself, and its decisive social groups, become aware of those new alternatives and are capable of doing so in general.

m.g. We already touched on this question to some extent, Zdeněk, when we talked about the fact that reform in the Soviet system could only have begun "from the top down." After all a totalitarian regime had existed here for decades, a regime that did not allow any social group other than the one in power to formulate its ideas about political and social development. Worse yet, even within the ruling group any "deviation" from "the only truth" was persecuted. The dogmas of the ruling ideology were considered to be "the only truth." Even within the framework of party ideology different viewpoints and discussion were not permitted, because pluralism of opinions "did not correspond to the interests of the workers." Compromise, that is, resolving a dispute in any way other than by suppressing one side of it, was considered not a principled way of doing things; it was considered defective behavior in politics, and in extreme cases, even a political crime.

Nevertheless there were different social strata, different groups and individuals, whose interests and views, sometimes on fundamental questions, came into conflict with the prevailing system. But all such things, as I said, were nipped in the bud. We were deprived of any mechanism for the expression and political resolution of conflicts and contradictions, mechanisms that in democratic countries transform such conflicts into a source of forward movement, rather than a source of crisis for the system. As a result the presence of contradictions, and the disparate needs and interests of people, in our country led only to isolated, fragmented, or hidden forms of disagreement or protest. There was no way they could manifest themselves in a systematic elaboration of alternative conceptions for the development of society, or in political programs. And of course the very idea of the necessity for, or usefulness of, a political opposition was not permitted in Soviet society.

Z.M. Yes, in the Soviet system people were denied the choice of an opportunity to express themselves "for" or "against" one or another conception of development. But it was precisely under those conditions that it proved necessary to begin perestroika. The inevitable result was that highly varied ideas and proposals, which until then had not been discussed and therefore were often not fully developed, appeared on the stage of practical politics. Hundreds and thousands of complex and contradictory specific problems entered the political field without having been part of any previously worked-out political conception.

M.G. Yes, Zdeněk, from the very beginning we had to act on a moment's notice, in the midst of life as we knew it, to open a path for pluralism of opinions, to develop glasnost and provide more democracy in order to overcome the previous lack of any alternative in the life and thinking of our society. And only in the process of these practical changes did there begin to appear in our public and political life various and sometimes quite unclear conceptions about the future. But any society that wants to develop along the road of political pluralism must inevitably acquire some positive historical experience in applying the principles of pluralism. After all, that was how the course of historical development took place in the West, and many long years were required for that—entire historical epochs. In the context of historical conditions in our country much more time was needed than the short six years of perestroika.

So then, the question of whether our society will have the possibility of a democratic search for alternative ways of development has not yet been decided. And even today I consider that the most important thing: to preserve the possibility of choosing freely among various alternative paths. This of course presupposes actual preconditions for various social interests to be expressed and for functioning democratic instruments to be established to protect or defend such interests. For democratic politics to once again be subordinated to some sort of "truth decided by the highest body"—which would still depend on a specific ideological content—I consider that the greatest threat today, just as it was at the beginning of perestroika.

z.m.   In my opinion, Misha, you are absolutely right about that. In history various ideologies quite different in content have played the role of a brake on the development of democracy and pluralism of opinion. These have varied from religious to nationalist and from revolutionary to counterrevolutionary. The experience of Lenin himself showed that once pluralism of opinion is suppressed, even a "class-based democracy" cannot be saved by attempts to draw the "mass of the workers" directly into politics.

m.g.   Here I must again return to 1983, when I was preparing my report on the anniversary of Lenin's birth. I made a kind of new discovery for myself at that time: it seemed to me that I began to understand the essence of Leninism as an attempt to develop in practice the "living creative activity of the masses." This creative activity at the same time seemed to me impossible without democracy, without the expression of differing views and the clash of those views, that is, pluralism and freedom of choice.

z.m.   With that understanding of Leninism you remained much more of a solitary figure than you yourself realized. Besides that, during perestroika it was also inevitable that, given a pluralism of views, people would appear who totally rejected not only Leninism but also the socialist orientation in general. But let us return to the question of the role of Soviet intellectuals in the process of formulating alternative concepts for the development of Soviet society.

M.G.   Our intellectuals working in the sciences and the arts had essentially more freedom after Stalin's death than other social groups. This was distinctly expressed after 1956 not only in creative writing (up to and including publication of works by Solzhenitsyn) but also in the social sciences, beginning with philosophical discussions, going through critical historiography, and ending with many years of critical discussion among economists about planning and the market. At that time there began to develop a certain amount of cooperation with people outside the Soviet Union, especially with the authors of reformist conceptions in other socialist countries.

But after 1968, after the defeat of your attempt at reform, a period of reaction began in the realm of ideology. Reform-minded representatives of the intelligentsia were forced to hold their tongue. The authorities dealt unceremoniously with those who did not agree and they did not stop short of outright repression.

At the beginning of perestroika the moods among the intellectuals changed sharply. A significant number came out in support of perestroika, but something unexpected happened—there was no shortage of criticism of the past, but the elaboration of reform theories, which is really what perestroika needed, was on a much smaller scale, by several orders of magnitude, than the outburst of criticism.

Z.M.   However, various groups of experts did come forward with various recommendations, mainly in regard to economic policy. After all both the "500 days" program, which we've already mentioned, and the idea of "shock therapy," which Gaidar actually carried through later on, after your resignation and the dissolution of the USSR—all of that was born in the offices of intellectual experts and specialists. Thus, in my opinion, an essential role was played also by the generation of scholars and scientists who had originally been Marxists and were convinced of the possibility of revitalizing socialism, but as a result of everything you have discussed, lost that conviction or else were unable to make a connection between that conviction and critical analysis in their own field of specialization. The opposite was also true. Representatives of the younger generation, who were no longer confirmed Marxists and who had no faith in socialism, had sufficient audacity to present their proposals concerning what the new policies should be and how they should be carried out. If we are to summarize this in a certain way, we could say that, strictly speaking, their proposals came down to one idea: that Soviet society should as quickly as possible accept Western models. The results of this idea have turned out to be, as we see today, less than glorious, and what will ultimately come of it all, only the future can tell. But the claim can hardly be made that these people have succeeded, in contrast to the policies of perestroika, in landing the airplane of their policies in the place they wanted to.

Returning to the airplane metaphor, I think that if the airplane of perestroika had not taken off, the question of where Soviet society was going to "land" would never have come up. Because society would not have moved from dead center and would have continued to decompose under the cover of Brezhnev's stagnant pseudo stability.

No One Knows Where History Will "Land"

z.m.   If we stick with the analogy of the airplane whose crew doesn't know where they will land, it can be said that all of human history is analogous to such an airplane. Beginning with the time when cave people left their caves, and going through all the revolutions, counterrevolutions, and wars, up to and including the recent end of the Cold War and the beginning of the computer revolution, no one can say where human history will "land."

m.g.   Yes, if we think about this more deeply, we come to the conclusion that in the framework of politics no one, including those who might play a decisive role for decades, can answer the question that only the historical process itself can answer.

z.m.   The conservative critics of perestroika thought about this in a different way of course. They had very specific ideas. They were simply trying to say that you were carrying out policies but did not know where they would lead.

m.g.   Yes, by playing with these words they wanted to sow doubts in society concerning our reform policies.

The conception of perestroika was aimed at a profound qualitative change in society by linking socialism with democracy. That was the main goal, and it was a humane one. What historical length of time would have been necessary for this, what specific forms of social development would be required—only the practice of perestroika itself could provide the answer to those questions. When we began to understand that everything was much more complex than it had seemed at first, when we saw how strong the resistance of the *nomenklatura* was to the reforms, we of course had to make corrections in our policies while the process was already under way. But the goal and intention of our conception remained as it had been originally.

z.m.   Yes, but on this very point a question comes up. Doesn't politics always turn out to be, strictly speaking, the pursuit of the pragmatic interests of various social forces and of society as a whole? Didn't perestroika get transformed, then, into an attempt to make history directly? An attempt, so to speak, to make history in a blunt and forthright way, not going through the intermediation of political pragmatism—that is, an attempt to realize definite ideals, to clear the road for certain particular historical requirements. To the extent that a policy understands itself in this way, it measures the correctness of the steps it has taken not by its political successes or defeats but by whether it corresponds to strictly defined historical requirements. In essence this coincides with Lenin's original understanding of the relation between history and politics, although the political content is different than it was with Lenin.

This is not meant as criticism but as an attempt to explain the evident contradiction between how obvious the defeat of the policies of perestroika was (culminating in the dissolution of the USSR) and how great at the same time its merits were, what it achieved by opening up new possibilities for historical development on the eve of a new millennium.

All this is still an open historical process, and it is not our business to pass final judgment. Neither political successes nor political failures were ever the proof of the historical correctness of a policy. After all, even Nazism for many years seemed to be a political success in a certain sense. Therefore, I understand your conviction that the criterion for the correctness of a policy is the kind of historical development it contributes to or, on the contrary, becomes a hindrance to. If you had not been profoundly convinced of this, you would never have found the strength necessary to carry through perestroika.

5. WHAT TO DO WITH THE PARTY?

Z.M.   In the attempt to fundamentally change a system of the Soviet type there was always a very important question: What role in this process ought to be played by the Communist Party, which had a monopoly on power? We both began as reformers within such a party, and we both based ourselves on the idea that the process of reform and of systemic changes must begin first of all within the Communist Party and under its leadership. I think that really was an essential precondition, so that systemic changes would not immediately, from the very beginning, result in explosions of the accumulated contradictions, so that the changes would not begin with the collapse of the existing structures rather than the reform of those structures leading gradually toward democratization. Of course, people who considered the collapse of the Soviet system a necessary starting point for change never shared this view. But neither of us belonged to that category. And therefore today, when the downfall of the Soviet system has actually occurred, it would be worthwhile for each of us to try to present his

concept of the role of the Communist Party in the transition from totalitarianism to democracy.

M.G.   I was deeply convinced that reform had to begin in the party. I based this view on my knowledge of our country and society, and the machinery of state, whose nucleus and support structure unquestionably was the CPSU. It was not a political party in pure form, although those who want to say that it was not a party at all are also wrong. Because it did have many rank-and-file units, or structures at the base, containing millions of people. This specific organism was a product of the system. I understood that without reform ideas being accepted within the party itself, without the party itself leading the reform processes, nothing could be accomplished in our country and fundamental changes in general could not be started. And I can see today that that was a correct conclusion.

Z.M.   What you are talking about now is something I tried to formulate in my theoretical analysis of the ruling Communist parties. I argued that these parties were many-sided, that they had, not just one, but multiple social functions. To put it in a highly oversimplified way, they were both the creators and the products of the system of totalitarian power, but at the same time they were the key to changing it. They had created the means of ideological defense or protection of this system, seeking to legitimize and justify it, but at the same time for that very reason, ideological criticism of the whole system could come into being inside these parties. They formed the connecting link for the whole system because of their practical activity, but precisely for that reason the whole system could be changed by making use of the impact these parties could have on society. In a political-organizational sense these parties comprised not only the ruling elite but also approximately 15 percent of the adult population. Hence, when we talk about the party, we should always distinguish between the party as the decisive mechanism of totalitarian power and as a distinct social organism. It was also an indispensable tool for the system, because it enabled the

manipulation of millions of people in nonpolitical professions and social roles.

Ideas and Realities

M.G.   Precisely this dual character of the party was more and more
distinctly expressed in the process of perestroika. The party as the
mechanism of totalitarian power—to simplify things, I will talk only
about the *nomenklatura*—never expressed enthusiasm about the development of democracy, glasnost, etc., because it clearly realized that
all this would place it under the control of society. But its domination
over the course of decades had been based on concealing truthful information about the situation in the country. As glasnost developed a
large part of the *nomenklatura* began to express dissatisfaction in regard to revelations about the real practices of the ruling power both
in the past and in the present. The *nomenklatura* realized that writers,
scholars, scientists, and above all journalists were beginning to pose
all sorts of current, vital questions in an open way—they regarded that
as the weakening of their own control over these elements and over
society as a whole.

And so the slogan adopted at the beginning by the entire party (both
as a social organism and as a mechanism of power), namely, that the
initiating and driving force of perestroika was and must be the Communists and their party, was in practice carried out inconsistently, although millions of Communists, despite the mechanism of power, were
in favor of the new policy. They often did not know how to carry it
out and besides without the party structure, without the apparatus and
the *nomenklatura*, they were, strictly speaking, powerless. The party
itself as a mechanism of power, and a large part of the *nomenklatura*,
became a barrier, an obstruction on the road to reform.

Z.M.   When did you first begin to understand that there was beginning to be a divergence—and in a dangerous form—between your
original conception of the role of the party and the actual reality?

M.G.   I would say as early as the end of 1986, and that was why the CPSU Central Committee Plenum was held in January 1987; also, later, after the Party Conference in 1998; then more and more distinctly, in a new and even threatening form, after the elections of 1989.

I was traveling around the Soviet Union a great deal then, and from my own experience I became convinced that everywhere, starting in the Far East and going to the southernmost provinces of Russia and Ukraine, the situation was one and the same: the party was becoming a brake on perestroika.

Z.M.   The party in the sense of its bureaucratic apparatus, the *nomenklatura*, but not all the nearly twenty million members. . . .

M.G.   Yes, the apparatus. But without it the party ceased to be an effective political force. The section of official cadres that accepted perestroika and began to show initiative in their work more and more often encountered opposition from the party *nomenklatura*. They would openly tell people: "There's no hurry! These 'reformers' come and go. How many of them we've seen in the past." In early 1987 a difficult battle inside the CPSU between the reformers and the anti-reform wing began. This conflict and confrontation permeated all the structures of society. After all, the Communists were present everywhere.

At the end of 1987, in my report on the 70th anniversary of the October revolution, I opened the way for a further and more profoundly critical approach to the past and to the present day. The Soviet intellectuals actively joined in on this process of criticism. Unfortunately, at the same time it became fashionable to condemn everything publicly and in as radical a way as possible, beginning with October 1917 and ending with the role of the party in the policy of perestroika. In society there arose a great confusion in people's minds. The party *nomenklatura*, seeking to use all of this in its own interests, made new attempts to put the brakes on change. It became clear that if we didn't win over the citizenry for active support of perestroika and if at the same time a separation of the party from the mechanism of totalitarian power did not take place, the policy of perestroika would be endangered.

z.m.   One could object at this point, however, that you, after all, could have proposed such a separation, and that was precisely because you knew the mechanism of power so well. From my own experience in 1968 I can say that, at that time, we reform Communists took into account the resistance of a certain section of the *nomenklatura* inside the party. But evidently it is also true that the conditions in the CPC then and the state of affairs in the CPSU during perestroika were fairly different. Not only did the traditions and political culture in Czechoslovakia and the USSR differ from one another, but also the times had changed, and the generations that were playing the decisive role were different. We have already talked about this, but it may be possible to speak about it again quite briefly—namely, that in our country in 1968 representatives of the generation that had gone through the experience of the prewar crisis, that had survived the war and Stalin's dictatorship, were the people who played the decisive role. They believed that all that was a thing of the past and that socialism really could be revitalized and given a "human face." After all, in 1970 one-third of all members of the CPC were expelled from the party because they disagreed with suppression of the reforms. Among them were many people from the *nomenklatura*. I would say that approximately 40 percent were officials of the *nomenklatura*.

Of course it will never be possible to say with certainty how the CPC of that time might have conducted itself if there had not been military intervention. But we can assume that the conditions for a reform policy then were better inside our party than in the CPSU a quarter of a century later. The Prague Spring was not a reform carried out under compulsion. It grew up among representatives of the middle generation in the party at that time (and partially within the society as a whole), on the soil of hopes and beliefs in their own abilities and powers, and the belief that socialism could be linked up with modern European society and consequently with democracy.

But when you became the head of the party, Misha, everything

looked different. Either you would succeed in putting an end to the stagnation and corruption of the Brezhnev era or you'd be threatened with complete collapse, especially because of the unbearable burden of arms spending. Thus, reform had become a compelling need.

M.G.   Yes, that's exactly right. But to touch on the analogy with the Prague Spring of 1968 again, I want to add something essential. For us to begin reform in 1985 was something quite different from the reform effort in Czechoslovakia. We, that is, the Soviet Union, constituted the nucleus of the socialist camp, one of the two major blocs in the world. Absolute discipline was required of us; the slightest deviation from the established line was considered betrayal. For the general secretary to undertake reform under such conditions—that was something unheard of. Reform could also not begin with someone announcing that pluralism was necessary. That would have been a totally nonsensical idea. One could only begin with the economy, raising the demand to overcome economic backwardness and to accelerate economic development. Under those conditions I said again and again that the party must lead the entire process. In contrast to the past, the role of discipline, order, and so forth was emphasized. To tell the truth, many of the official cadres did not think that their situation would change or that the demands placed on them in their official areas of work would change in any radical way; they didn't think that in the course of democratic processes they would be placed under the control of society. When that happened many of those who initially accepted the need for change began to offer resistance.

Z.M.   I remember how you yourself thirty years earlier reacted against the policies of Khrushchev. At first you were a confirmed supporter of his polices; later it began to seem to you that Khrushchev was no longer in control of things, was senselessly rushing from one extreme to another, destroying the party, dividing it into "industrial" and "agricultural" branches, and so forth. For that reason in the end you took a positive attitude toward his removal from his post. And don't you think that during the course of perestroika more than one provincial party secretary reasoned in a way similar to the way in which a onetime secretary of the Stavropol committee, Gorbachev, had reasoned? Why didn't you draw the conclusion from this that it would be better to slow down the pace of change, in a certain way to "wait for the party," which had lagged behind the pace of change in the society as a whole?

M.G.   Of course, I knew that some young party secretaries might base themselves on the same kind of considerations that the young secretary of the Stavropol committee had once done. But I also understood that the same fate that had befallen Khrushchev could be waiting for us, along with our policy of perestroika. I understood this very clearly in 1987, when I saw that our reforms, just like those in the Khrushchev era, were having a seriously painful effect on the interests of the *nomenklatura*, that is, on the party as a mechanism of power. I proposed to unravel this knotty problem through political reform. That is, to place the *nomenklatura* in the position where it could show itself under new circumstances, acquire new methods, and demonstrate that it was capable of functioning under democratic control! In doing this I repeated insistently: "We will give all officials a chance to restructure themselves. But whoever cannot or does not want to accept the new conditions of political work must leave."

Zdeněk, you've just said that I should have slowed down the pace of change, to wait for the party to mature to the point of understanding the necessity of change, the absence of any alternative to change. But I did exactly that, and immediately came under criticism not only from the radical intellectuals but also, and quite sharply, from ordinary citizens. They suspected me of making a deal with the *nomenklatura*.

Z.M.   But it was precisely the comrades who were used to giving orders and taking advantage of their positions as officials of the *nomenklatura* who were never going to retire voluntarily.

M.G.   That is why it was necessary to create mechanisms that would force the party as an apparatus of totalitarian power to subordinate itself to the needs of perestroika and to democratic rules. In other words, the party had to either cease playing the role of a mechanism of totalitarian power or the entire new policy would be mortally endangered. The reason for which individuals or particular groups came out against the policy of perestroika was a secondary question from the point of view of our policies as a whole. It was not possible to regulate the pace of change by taking that into account. Moreover, at the time, real changes in society outside of the party had a substantially more significant effect on tempo and timing than decisions by party bodies. The party was obviously lagging behind, and the farther we went, the more it lagged—that was the problem.

Separating the Party from the State

z.m.   My experiences, and my reflections on them, were the same. At a certain phase of democratic reform it's necessary without fail to achieve a certain end. That is, to see to it that within the party, in the form of its official bodies and apparatus, there would not arise any centers that in fact would have unlimited power, that could take any decisions they wanted without having to answer for their actions. A decisive step in this direction could be taken only by separating the party from the state. That means party bodies and the apparatus must lose their de facto power of making decisions in advance that affect the course of administration of the economy and government instead of those decisions being made by the elected government bodies.

But to achieve this goal and not to cause chaos in the management of public affairs or a revolt by the *nomenklatura*, which would be losing the very basis of its existence during this process—that is the main test for any and all reform policies. In any case, the very beginning of the process leading toward this goal is the most dangerous moment for reform. The extraordinary complexity of this whole set of problems increases also because it is not only a matter of eliminating undemocratic influence by the central government; at the same time the leadership must provide itself with truly democratic bodies, so that a dictatorship by Communist autocrats would not simply be replaced by a dictatorship of non-Communist or anti-Communist autocrats.

M.G.   In the actions we took we had to keep in mind our knowledge
of the system. Thus, the very first steps were aimed at strengthening
the position of the reformers in the Politburo, and that was accomplished. Then we needed glasnost to create the kind of atmosphere in
society that would correspond to the needs of perestroika. Life itself
led us to an understanding of the fact that without modernization of
the mechanism of power it would be difficult for us to move the reforms forward, and this had to be done at a time when no strong front
of resistance had yet arisen. That time came, in my opinion, in 1987.
The slogan placed on the order of the day was "All power to the Soviets!" The intention here was to place party officials from the structures of actual *nomenklatura* power under the control of society. These
officials would have to prove, through elections, that they had real
abilities and the right to occupy their leading positions.

But in this case also—and you must know this—I acted through the
party and with its consent. Thus, instead of a forcible change of party
officials carried out by some sort of monitoring bodies or investigative
agencies there was the *test of elections*. I spoke at the Nineteenth CPSU
Conference on all these problems. After sharp debate the conference
approved the entire package of proposals, whose adoption opened the
door for political reform. But from that moment resistance to reform
began to take on a very definite shape.

Z.M.   In general it's understandable that the Stalinists in the party
would begin to defend themselves. But this did not necessarily have to
mean failure for the reforms. I was especially interested in a criticism
Ryzhkov made, in his memoirs, of the slogan "All Power to the Soviets." He interpreted what was being done in practice as a desire to
subordinate skilled specialists and the professional apparatus to the
political orders of apparatchiks of the moment who won office on the
basis of cheap and unrealistic promises to voters. He considered this
the strengthening of groups in the party apparatus that would later
carry out a policy of dictating to specialists, concealing their arbitrary
ways under the guise of the "will of the people." At the same time
Ryzhkov proudly declares that the Council of Ministers, which he

headed and which had been founded on new principles, with each of its members being separately confirmed by the Supreme Soviet—that this was the first truly independent government in the USSR, or so he claims. He himself was pleased by the fact that as head of the Council of Ministers he was not subordinated to the party apparatus. But the conclusion can be drawn from his criticism that the slogan "All Power to the Soviets" turned many against your policies, not just the party *nomenklatura*, but a significant section of the influential technocrats, above all the professionally educated ones in the economic apparatus.

M.G.   Giving all power to the Soviets meant first of all freedom from party dictates not only for elected government bodies but also for executive bodies established by those legislative bodies. It meant a law-based separation of government powers. For now I won't talk about the extent to which Soviet government bodies turned out to be capable (or not) of assuming the responsibility that the party previously had. It is of no small importance that the new government formed by the Supreme Soviet (elected in 1989) also received its mandate from that body, as Nikolai Ryzhkov said. But the main thing is that from then on both the head of the government and his colleagues in the cabinet began to exercise independence and to reject interference in their work by party bodies, especially the Secretariat of the Central Committee and the party apparatus in general. I cannot agree with Ryzhkov's arguments on how politics and economics interact. Contradictions arise between them. That's normal. Politics is the instrument through which the varying interests in society are made evident and adjusted and coordinated. Politics puts forward certain programmatic aims which economics is obliged to take into account. Often politics and policies are bad, and are rejected by the citizens. In that case sooner or later new policies come to replace the old ones. Ryzhkov's arguments are a reaction against politics and represent a technocratic view of policy making. And well, after all, at a certain stage of the reforms under perestroika there was a convergence between sections of the party *nomenklatura* and the administrative and managerial officials who did not agree with the changes infringing on their material interests. Undoubtedly that did happen, and it greatly complicated the process of reform.

Z.M.   The idea of a new political system was embodied in the directives issued by the Nineteenth Party Conference of the CPSU. These provided for a Congress of People's Deputies, which in turn would elect a Supreme Soviet, and corresponding election laws made those bodies possible. Many people who supported perestroika considered all this merely a temporary measure, part of a search for the right road. In the end the real separation of the party from the government presupposed a whole series of further steps, primarily the consistent introduction of all the principles of government by law and of course the creation of social organizations independent of the Communist Party, and so forth. In short, such a separation could be realized only in a pluralistic political system.

M.G.   Yes, of course that was only the beginning of an entire process. But without the mechanism of the Congresses of People's Deputies, and without elections in which there were several candidates to choose from, not just one, it would have been completely impossible to maintain the policy of overcoming the totalitarian nature of political power in our country. This brought many new people into our political structures to take their place alongside representatives of the old *nomenklatura*. But the process of taking power out of the hands of the party as a mechanism of power was still far from being completed. It had only begun. For that reason, also for me personally at the time, there was no other solution than to keep the highest level of party and government authority in my own hands. Otherwise, there would have been a loss of decisive influence on the actual mechanism of power.

Political Pluralism—the Aim and Instrument of Perestroika

Z.M.   I will start once again with 1968 in Czechoslovakia. The main aim was to remove monopoly domination by the Communist Party and arrive at a pluralistic democratic system. I saw that as the main

thing, just as you did after 1987. Of course our situation then had the fundamental difference that we had to be constantly alert to what Moscow would say. That is why we were afraid to do one thing or another, so as not to get into experiments that were "impermissible" under Cold War conditions. In your case everything was different. With your policy of perestroika you made fundamental changes precisely in international relations, and the situation of being watched over by a foreign power was not constantly hanging over you. That was a huge advantage for you, but sometimes it was probably also a disadvantage, because in our case our situation forced us to move cautiously and this kept us from becoming too self-assured.

In 1968 when I reflected upon the possibility of a pluralist system I thought, however—and this was aside from any consideration of what would be said about it in the Kremlin—that it would be impossible to begin by granting permission for the formation of new political parties, which would then compete with the CPC for power through free elections. I held the view that in such a case it would not be a reform, but political suicide. A fundamental change of the system might culminate in competition in elections among various political parties, but it could not begin that way. Our thinking was that this could become realistic only after eight to ten years.

But we didn't want to spend all those years passively waiting for the onset of political pluralism, because it was not only an aim but also a means, an instrument of democratic reform. In the first stage I considered it possible to permit freedom of the press and competing opinions, to allow various social groups to publicly take their stands and participate in making political decisions through social organizations (the trade unions, youth organizations, women's organizations) as well as bodies of local self-government in cities, towns, and regions, self-management bodies made up of the work forces at factories, etc. And only later when these forms of pluralism had weakened the force of the accumulated contradictions would society become used to acting democratically in the sphere of political practice. Only then did I admit the possibility of free elections in which both ruling and opposition political parties would take part.

In the meantime, in the CPC itself various ideological tendencies, platforms, or factions would have developed, and internal party life would no longer be subordinated to the principles of "democratic centralism." The party would gradually become a political organism of the Social Democratic type, but in the framework of the reform program that had been adopted. Non-Communist political parties that already existed or had newly arisen would in the first stage have to remain tied politically and organizationally to the framework of the National Front and its reform program. Of course this was a glaring restriction on political pluralism, but for all that, it still was pluralism; it would not have been a totalitarian, but a democratic system.

Basically this would have been a revival of the model of the political system in Czechoslovakia in the years 1945–48. The National Front had not been a monopoly held by any one party by itself. It was a fairly broad government coalition; that is, internally it was pluralistic. But it had been a form of government that did not allow parties to take part in elections unless they belonged to the front. Such a limitation of party pluralism I considered a necessary condition so that the old system would not fall apart all at once, but would truly be reformed in a gradual way. But to do the opposite, to begin with the possibility of the anti-Communist opposition competing for the majority in elections, would mean to begin the destruction of the entire system, the overthrow of the government instead of reform. And that could have happened even in 1968 in Czechoslovakia, after twenty years of dictatorship by the CPC, in spite of the mass support for the reform Communists.

It was on all this that I based my views when you and I talked in February 1990 about whether the emergence of new political parties, a system with a government party and an opposition party, should be allowed in the USSR. I said then that that would mean letting the genie out of the bottle and that before that, as soon as possible, it would be necessary to develop other forms and structures of pluralism and also, of chief importance, to find a way of ensuring that the work collectives would begin to play an important political role. You agreed with me in principle then, but later developments took a different path, and in

spite of every thing a multiparty system came into being in the USSR very quickly. What kind of pressures came to bear in this situation? And what was your understanding of the development of political pluralism within the framework of perestroika?

M.G.   For all the logic of your arguments, you and I cannot say exactly how all this would have worked out in real life. All one needs to do is recall the summer of 1968. In comparison to the spring in Prague, it had already become something different. Moreover, I doubt that as the process developed you could have succeeded in regulating it in such a way as to arrive at political pluralism and the establishment of opposition parties only after ten years. No, they simply would have arisen on their own. Let me answer one question (briefly): How did we come to a conclusion favoring the recognition of political pluralism?

In our case the reform began as an attempt to extricate our country from economic stagnation, not as a desire for pluralism. Later developments in many respects transpired under the impact of new circumstances. The starting point for perestroika was the recognition of the need to let democracy unfold (to combine socialism and democracy). This quickly, and moreover sharply, posed the question of political pluralism. At first we had to accept pluralism of opinions. My reasoning then was that a multiparty system was neither an inevitable symptom nor a proof of democracy. There are countries where dictatorship prevails in spite of a multiparty system. In our country, in the USSR, we could do the opposite, accomplish the expression of various interests within the framework of our system if democracy could exist inside the party and if various social organizations and organizations of the creative intelligentsia were developed further, along with self-management. That is what I said during the period when social organizations were given access to power, participation in government, by allowing them a quota of a certain number of delegates at Congresses of People's Deputies and higher Soviet bodies. Then despite the existence of only one party, it would already be possible for other organizations to find a way of exerting political influence.

But at that very time, when all that had been carried out, I saw that

it was insufficient, that developments had gone farther. Both inside the
Congress of People's Deputies and in other areas of public life various
ideological tendencies and groupings had begun to arise. It was impossible not to take into consideration the so-called Interregional
Group of Deputies. And in the fall of 1989 political parties began to
make their appearance one after the other—or rather, strictly speaking,
these were only embryonic forms of oppositional parties. At that time
I no longer excluded the possibility of development along those lines.
More than that, I began to think that this could become a base of
support in a conflict with the *nomenklatura*. Because inside the party
itself a process of differentiation had already begun, and at least five
political tendencies had emerged.

That was also the time when there arose at the center of public
discussion the question of making changes in an article of the Soviet
Constitution that dealt with the CPSU. The celebrated Article 6, which
codified the ruling and directing role of the CPSU in society. Some
people criticized me then for delaying the solution of that problem,
while others demanded the opposite—that the question be taken off
the agenda completely. My thinking was that the initiative in this matter should come from the CPSU Central Committee itself, that it should
rise to the occasion. That actually is what happened later. Besides that,
I made a connection between annulment of Article 6 and the establishment of the institution of the presidency. And as you know, that is
how we proceeded. But when the changes were made in the constitution a fierce debate broke out among the delegates over whether clauses
should be added to the fundamental law of our country on the question
of political parties. Despite all the cautious wording of the clauses that
were adopted they opened the road to political pluralism. And the free
elections that were held in the spring of 1990 in the republics of the
USSR speeded up this process sharply.

Z.M.   But in reality these developments resulted not in the emergence
of a workable system of several parties but rather in the decomposition
of the CPSU into various factions and tendencies and the rise of pseudo

parties. Neither then nor later did this have anything in common with the Western type of pluralism.

M.G.   In Russia in this case also the process of the emergence of parties will not simply copy the West. And as far as the Communist Party is concerned, the process of differentiation inside it had begun, as I have said, much earlier. The Nineteenth Conference of the CPSU made it possible to mobilize the party as a social organism, and it was this party that—in spite of the apparatus and in spite of the *nomenkla-tura*—succeeded in taking a stronger line in support of perestroika and the broad development of democracy, that is, the introduction of political reform. The aim I pursued was that the various tendencies that were arising should each take on its own organizational and, later, legal form. What I also wanted to achieve was that it would become possible to develop the party as a social organism, that is, to regroup and reshape the millions of Communists who were not part of the *nomenklatura*.

Could Gorbachev Have Founded a New Party?

Z.M.   A question then arises, one that can sometimes be heard even today: Wouldn't it have been better in general for you to have begun the development in the direction of pluralism by founding your own party, consisting of the reform elements in the CPSU? I myself, as you know, did not share that view. On the contrary, I thought that the combining of the highest party post and highest governmental post in your person was a condition for you to retain actual power and to be able to use it for the sake of the new policies. But today, when everything has ended up quite differently from what we expected, how do you see all that, looking back?

M.G.   There were many who advised me to leave my post as general secretary of the party so that I could stand above the disputing sides and from the high reaches of presidential power go on and carry out the policies of perestroika. But I was trying to achieve something quite different; through my actions I wanted to contribute to the aim that the strength of the party, without which nothing at all could be done, should take the side of perestroika.

I think that during the Twenty-Eighth Congress of the CPSU in 1990 my leaving the highest party post would have been an outright gift to all the opponents of perestroika. The party as a mechanism of power still had control of everything then, elections had just taken place, and other political parties and organizations were only in the process of formation. The *nomenklatura*, on the other hand, already understood that the bell was tolling for it, and it began to go on the offensive.

z.m.   One of your closest assistants, Chernyaev, writes in his memoirs that he along with others, for example, Alexander Yakovlev, considered it correct for you to resign as general secretary then. In their opinion you should have withdrawn, just as Yeltsin had earlier. By doing so, he had succeeded in strengthening his political positions. If you at that time, the argument goes, had become completely independent as president, you could have won those political positions instead of Yeltsin, and everything could have come out quite differently. Chernyaev asserts that you remained at the head of the party, aside from everything else, because you still believed in the "socialist choice," although your advisers even then viewed your decision as a product of your indecisiveness and overly emotional approach.

m.g.   I have already spoken many times, Zdeněk, about the difference between taking advice and taking responsibility for decisions that have been made, and so I do not want to return to that subject. I did not want to, and I could not have, conducted myself the way Yeltsin did. The game he was playing ended up with the dissolution of the USSR. For me Yeltsin was never an example to be followed, but rather the opposite. If I made an alliance with him, it was solely out of political considerations. As for the socialist choice, I did not conceal the fact that I always sought solutions that would correspond to my ideas in that regard, ideas that, incidentally, underwent profound change. What

other people thought about that is their problem, and they will have to answer for that themselves. Let me repeat, the aim I strove for then was to keep the main forces of the party in support of perestroika and to damp down and weaken confrontation, which already contained the threat of potential conflict, as actually happened later, in August 1991. In the summer of 1990 antidogmatic forces had already gathered around the Democratic Platform, but unfortunately, left radicalism prevailed there. The opponents of perestroika were energetically laying the groundwork for a split in the party, because that still could have meant victory for them then. Serious consequences followed from the founding of the Communist Party of the Russian Federation, the leadership of which was taken by representatives of the conservative tendencies opposed to perestroika. At the head of their party they placed a typical representative of the *nomenklatura*, Polozkov. If I had retired from my post then, the reformers in the CPSU would have ended up in a minority. Many people say: "What of it? Society was still in favor of perestroika!" That's true. But again and again I must repeat: power had not yet been transferred from the hands of the party *nomenklatura*. People everywhere still went to get their orders and directions from the secretaries of the district party committees and regional party committees. Under such conditions the party as a mechanism of totalitarian power was still completely controlled by the conservative *nomenklatura*.

Z.M.   But after the Twenty-Eighth Congress, from the summer of 1990 to the summer of 1991, what about that? Wouldn't a division of the CPSU under your leadership at that time have prevented developments that later led to the attempt to remove you in August 1991?

M.G.   That was one of the periods that required the greatest responsibility not only as far as the development of the CPSU was concerned but also the reforming of the USSR. The possibility of splitting the CPSU and founding a new party striving for democratic socialism was never just a subject for theoretical reflection. It was a problem interconnected with the overall situation in the country. In the spring of

1991, before the April plenum of the CPSU Central Committee, an unconcealed struggle for power had already begun, and the forces seeking to remove Gorbachev were plainly evident. On the one hand, there was the anti-perestroika *nomenklatura* in the CPSU and, on the other, there was Yelstin, who was then chairman of the Supreme Soviet of the Russian Federation. This was not a personal struggle; it was a struggle over the further development of perestroika. I sought to prevent the development of a conflict that might endanger the very existence of the Soviet Union and create the possibility of civil war. I did everything I could to keep things within the framework of the constitution and legality and to resolve questions that arose by political methods on the basis of negotiation and compromise. My task, as I saw it, was not to let myself be provoked and not to retreat from the approach I have described.

In March 1991 a question arose of a vote of confidence in Yeltsin at the Congress of People's Deputies of the RSFSR. I was in favor of him being relieved of his duties because he had used his position to increase tensions and worsen the situation in the country and in a number of cases he had resorted to the outright instigation of conflicts. At a decisive moment in this struggle at the congress Rutskoi organized a group of deputies under the name "Communists for Democracy," which took Yeltsin's side, while the leader of the Communist Party of the Russian Federation, Polozkov, withdrew his demand that Yeltsin be recalled. Polozkov felt that he was being used to promote the interests of the central government (as against the Russian Federation). The status quo was preserved (that is, Yeltsin was not removed) and I had to deal with that as a fact of life.

Not only that. It was precisely after that congress, and taking the political realities into account, that I held the meeting at Novo-Ogarevo with the leaders of nine republics of the Soviet Union (including the Russian Federation, headed by Yeltsin). The purpose of the meeting was to begin a process of preparing a new Union Treaty. Because of that I was able to take an aggressive line at the Central Committee plenum. At that plenum there were crude and direct attacks on me, and a demand could be heard essentially that I should declare a state of emergency in the country or else resign from my post. And although I made a statement about resignation at that time, it was unacceptable to me, nevertheless, at that moment to bring things to the point of a split in the CPSU and the founding of a new party. A new congress of the CPSU would be necessary for a thing like that. A draft program was adopted at the Central Committee plenum in July 1991, and whoever reads it now will see that it was already a program for another party, a program of democratic socialism in the modern sense of the word. It was a break from the Stalinist Communism of the past. The August coup prevented a congress of the CPSU from being held in the fall. The party brought its own existence to an end.

z.m.   But if that had not happened, had you already made the decision internally that you would organize a new party at the next congress on the basis of that program?

m.g.   Yes. I had definite information that between 5 and 7 million members of the CPSU would have gone over to the new party.

What Can and Cannot Be Forbidden by Law

z.m.   But in reality everything turned out differently. There was no success in trying to transform a substantial part of the CPSU into a new, democratic socialist party in time. Before a new congress could carry out a "surgical operation" to remove the *nomenklatura* mechanism of totalitarian power from the body of the party, the top ranks of the *nomenklatura* in the party and government tried to remove you from power and to put a stop to your perestroika. The tried and true methods were applied—proclaiming a state of emergency and the use of police and military forces—but those old mechanisms could no longer succeed under the new circumstances. I think that, owing to everything I experienced in August 1968, I can imagine your situation at the time, probably much better than a number of other people. I myself was in the position of a person who lived for politics and in the name of politics. This person, you could say, was at the summits of power and then by a bolt of lightning his greatest political and personal hopes were smashed. I was in the position of a person who sees the results of his efforts of a lifetime being destroyed by barbarous violence on the part of those from whom he may have expected many insults and much persecution but not such a hare-brained adventure, not such thick-headedness and outright treason. A person who then had to consider all possibilities, up to and including the gallows, who then suddenly sees that violence has been forced to take a step backward and once again finds himself in the realm of political talks and negotiations. And all this he experiences over the course of two or three days. I know that at a time like that it seems to a person that his possibilities are much greater than they are in fact. It seems to him that the worst is now behind him and that the main thing will now depend on him, on his conduct and the political struggle, his skill in the art of negotiation and compromise. It was precisely in that kind of situation and in that frame of mind that I signed the Moscow Protocol in August 1968. Then for a quarter of a century I saw the results of that measure and experienced them as they affected my own person, and therefore I cannot console myself with the thought that this was not a capitulation by the Prague Spring itself. Despite that, however, to this day I do not have the inner certainty that back then I could have understood what a dead end resulted from our defeat, and consequently could have conducted myself differently. Your words and actions in the first days after your return to the Kremlin from being arrested in the Crimea—I am not capable of understanding them in any other way than from the point of view of my own experience back in 1968. Maybe that's wrong, but I simply can't do otherwise.

But I don't want to turn our conversation in that direction. I also don't want to repeat here what you have already written about August 1991, although we can hardly manage to avoid the subject completely. It would be worth talking about the question of what changed from the point of view of the prospects for democratic socialism in Russia by the de facto banning of the Communist Party and the question of what, on the other hand, no ban or prohibition by law can resolve.

M.G.   Before we begin talking about that question I would still like to say that it's impossible to understand and explain everything that happened back then if it is looked at from the outside and from a distance. One would have to find oneself in the specific situation I was in at the time. My return from house arrest in the Crimea was in my judgment a possibility for continuing the reforms within the framework of the choice that had been made. I spoke about that at my press conference. But in the course of the next two or three days it became clear to me that the Politburo had betrayed me, that the Central Committee Secretariat had betrayed me, and that the majority of regional party committee secretaries had also sided with the leaders of the coup.

Z.M.   Perhaps they were simply watching and waiting to see how it would all come out?

M.G.   Definitely not. They gave their support to the coup makers. That was the culmination of their resistance to perestroika, which had gradually ripened within the *nomenklatura*, as we have already discussed. I could no longer have negotiations with those people regarding future party work. For me, that was a painful drama because the party had not been an accidental episode in my life, and in my view the reformation of the party should have been carried through to the end. What weighed me down most of all, however, was the feeling of moral responsibility to people whose lives had been linked with the party and who had bound up their hopes with perestroika and had confidence in me personally.

Z.M.   All right, this has to do with your resignation from the post of general secretary of the CPSU. But there were a lot of other things. Above all, the session of the Supreme Soviet of the Russian Federation when Yeltsin forced you to be present in front of television cameras when he signed the decree banning the CPSU. Then there was the appeal to the CPSU Central Committee to dissolve itself, and your de facto consent to having the Central Committee building sealed, then

having these facilities taken away from the party and occupied by the
official bodies of the Russian Republic . . .

M.G.   Yes, that is a different story, and once again it is not all that
simple, but let's take these points in the proper order. In my statement resigning from the post of general secretary I gave the reasons
for my resignation. But at the same time I called upon all Communists
to exercise self-determination, to make their own decisions on what
position to take in regard to the events that had occurred. I based my
decision on my belief that the millions of party members should be
able to decide for themselves whether to take the side of the new
party program and whether they were for perestroika or against it.
What I strove for was that the party not be destroyed as a social
organism. . . .

Z.M.   However, as you yourself have rightly stated more than once,
the party members without the party apparatus and the organized bodies of the party were not in reality capable of taking action.

M.G.   Yes, that's also correct: the party committees and the party apparatus not only failed to lead the party members in a process of self-
determination but in fact made it impossible. But in that situation all
I could do was to appeal to party members.

As far as the Russian Supreme Soviet session goes, Yeltsin and I had
had a talk about the CPSU when we were on our way together to this
session. I said that under conditions of democracy all political tendencies have the right to exist. Yeltsin was thinking something, but it was
not clear what.

Then at the Supreme Soviet session in this extremely unusual way—
and after all, he does love to take measures that outwardly have a
dramatic effect—he decided to sign a decree banning activity by the
CPSU. I said that the most he could do was to suppress any activity
by party bodies or responsible officials who had supported the coup
until such time as this entire matter had been thoroughly investigated.

Yeltsin nevertheless signed the decree banning any activity by the CPSU as a whole.

z.m. Somewhat later, in a government resolution of November 6, 1991, on the eve of the anniversary of the October revolution, he went so far as to ban the party entirely. Only the Constitutional Court handed down a ruling corresponding to your initial views that banning the party was unconstitutional and asserting that only the activity of the ruling bodies of the party could be suppressed. But in fact, in the meantime, the situation had already amounted to a ban, and the CPSU was demolished both as a mechanism of power and as a social organism.

m.g. I no longer had any influence over that. Anyone who drew the conclusion that that was my point of view would not be right. As early as August at the same session of the Supreme Soviet of the Russian Federation I engaged in a sharp polemic against those who came forward with anti-Communist slogans. One of the deputies shouted hysterically, "Sweep all the Communists out of the country with a broom!" I answered, "You've blown your top: even Stalin's sick mind never went so far as to think up something like that." And I added: "Since you consider yourselves to be democrats, you should act accordingly."

z.m. But no one ever saw that on television or heard about it, and you never spoke of it yourself.

m.g. I have written about all of that and other things in my memoirs. But there is also a film in which all of this was recorded. But it's true that this has never been shown in full.

z.m. Well, in spite of all that, let's get back to our question: Whatever we call the end of the CPSU—its suppression, liquidation, or disintegration—what did that mean for the prospects of democratic socialism in Russia? I think that the answer to this question must be very contradictory. Because on the one hand it meant final emancipation from the mechanism of totalitarian power which portrayed itself as the embodiment of socialist principles, although it was the outright negation of any link between socialism and democracy. On the other hand, this created extraordinary complications for—and in fact for a time entirely ruled out—the possibility of building a strong political party fighting programmatically for democratic socialism. This means that a large number of people from various social groups had no real opportunity to render sufficiently effective political support to the policies of democratic socialism or social democracy, although broad social strata in a society of the Soviet type definitely had an interest in such a thing. For the socialist idea itself the downfall of the CPSU not only closed off the possibility of "revitalizing socialism" but also contributed to its being more greatly discredited later on.

M.G.   I don't want to repeat myself too much, but I would like to say once more that I did continue to fight to reform the CPSU up until the last moment. After my return from the Crimea I again defended the political goals embodied in the new CPSU program, and many people reproached me on the grounds that I didn't understand the depth of the changes that had taken place. But my reference to the new party program was not accidental: I wanted to provide a further impulse for Communists to move toward political self-determination.

Beginning in September 1991, and by now taking into account the changes in the country after the defeat of the August coup, I stated my views publicly several times. The model of socialism that had existed in our country had collapsed, but not the socialist idea itself. There were calls to "drive socialism out of our society." That I said was a utopia. No one could do that by passing a law or by some new crusade. It would be nothing more than the trampling of freedom of opinion and political pluralism underfoot.

In every country people should have the possibility of creating their own way of life and choosing it themselves. Within this framework they also have the hope of putting socialist ideas into practice. At the present time forces with a socialist and democratic orientation are greatly dispersed and fragmented in Russia, politically they are not very effective, and the petty disputes among them do them no good. Despite that, I think that in present-day Russia and in general on the territory of the former USSR they can take the initiative and play a decisive political role in preserving and developing democratic change in opposition to authoritarianism and fundamentalism of any kind.

Z.M.   Unfortunately, there is also the possible scenario of chaos in the realm of values and ideas, which populist demagogues of dictatorial bent could take advantage of. None of the possible variants of future development can progress without former members of the CPSU. The monopoly of that party lasted too long, just as the monopoly of the Catholic Church once did: anyone who took an active part in public life had to do so within the structures that were under the monopoly control of the Communist Party. Just as the Protestant Reformation in Western Europe could not have begun without Catholics and could not have made its way without them, so too Social Democratic ideas cannot win out in Russia today without former Communists. However, representatives of all other political variants, including nationalists and advocates of dictatorship, will also be fighting to influence these former Communists.

M.G.   In the specific situation in 1991 I considered that the chief condition for the long-term development of the Social Democratic orientation was preservation of the state based on a union of republics through the signing of a new Union Treaty. But the deal made by Yeltsin with Kravchuk and Shushkevich [presidents, respectively, of the Ukrainian and Belorussian republics] in December 1991 buried those hopes.

6. CAN THE USE OF FORCE "SAVE SOCIALISM"?

Z.M.   Misha, I think that it's clear from our entire preceding conversation that we hold a similar view to the effect that it would not have been possible to "save socialism" by a continuation of the Soviet system of "actually existing socialism," because that system really was not identical with socialism. Still less is it possible to "save socialism" by the use of force. Nevertheless, I would like to ask you this: If you look back on those years when you held supreme power in the USSR, doesn't it seem to you that government intervention (that is, ultimately the use of force) could have in certain specific situations prevented undesirable developments or, contrariwise, could have provided support for those tendencies and forces which were finally defeated, even though that was not in the interests of perestroika?

Violence Never Provides a Lasting Solution

M.G.   Decisions involving the use of force were for me a very intense drama that I was obliged to live through. From the very beginning of perestroika I proceeded on the basis that change must be carried out democratically through reforms and, most importantly, without bloodshed. My own experience, which I accumulated while holding the highest post in our government, showed unambiguously that the use of force as a method of long-term resolution of fundamental problems is unacceptable. It is hardly possible to rule out in the future the possibility in one or another country of revolutionary situations arising or sharp and abrupt turns of events. But those are not the things that will ensure the achievement of long-term goals in the final analysis; only reforms will do that. It can happen that in order to avoid a harsher use of force and even greater bloodshed, in order to separate the sides in a dispute, the necessity may arise for forcible intervention into a process of change. Such things happen in cases when there has been procrastination in politics or miscalculations have been made. But never, not once while I held the posts of general secretary and president, was there any confirmation that what I wanted could be achieved through the use of force.

Z.M.   All of that is true, but I could add to it just some additional arguments. For example, that the Soviet tanks in August 1968, from the point of view of long-term developments, achieved exactly the opposite result of what those who sent them said they wanted to achieve. And so, to try to hold together the "socialist camp" in 1989 with the use of force would undoubtedly not have "saved socialism." But if you survey the role of force or violence in history, and not just from the point of view of the Stalinist system, it is contradictory. You don't necessarily have to support Marx's proposition that violence is the midwife of progress in history. But it remains a fact that, for example, Lincoln rightly holds the position of one of the main democratic leaders in the history of the United States, although he resorted to violence without much hesitation in response to the attempts to break up the federation of states, and he waged a civil war from the North against the South. By this I do not at all mean to say that the Soviet Union might perhaps have been preserved by unleashing a war against the republics that wanted full independence. I only want to indicate that the use of force in history has by no means always contradicted the interests of democracy. Sometimes perhaps it has been quite the opposite. But in the USSR during perestroika it was impossible to try to preserve the union by that means. I agree with that.

M.G.   I don't think you can shake the foundations of my argument, based on present-day experience, by referring to the past history of the United States. First, an extra-historical approach is impermissible on this question. Granted that Lincoln remains a hero of his country and of his time. While granting him his due, I don't forget what the Civil War meant for people, what torments they had to undergo. Let us recall Margaret Mitchell's novel *Gone with the Wind*. What losses and sacrifices accompanied that war.

Second, I think that in our present discussions about the role of force we can't disregard the change in views on such a fundamental value as human life.

Finally, the attempted coup in August 1991, under the slogan of protecting and preserving the USSR, had exactly the opposite result: the disintegration of the union and expansion and intensification of conflicts on national or ethnic grounds in the post-Soviet space.

Who Wanted to Provoke Violence?

Z.M.   But let us return to our subject, the role of violence during perestroika.

M.G.   Beginning in late 1990 there was constant pressure on me to introduce presidential rule by decree or institute emergency measures in one or another region of the country. In March 1991 I gave in to the pressure and gave my consent for the government to introduce troops, including sending tanks to Moscow. But within a few hours I saw that this would only worsen the situation and that the danger which supposedly justified this measure did not in fact exist. All later attempts, and there were quite a few of them, to make me resort to the use of force were unsuccessful.

Z.M.   You were accused of the opposite, although without proof. Over and over again it was said—including outside the Soviet Union— that you supposedly agreed with the use of force in Tbilisi and in Lithuania. And of course the sending of troops to Baku.

M.G.   Yes, there was the case of Baku in January 1990. What was the situation there? There were mass pogroms against Armenians. Thousands of people were fleeing from the Azerbaijan Republic [whose capital was Baku], the border of the USSR [between the Azerbaijan Republic and neighboring Iran] was being destroyed, and people were seizing power in many regions with the use of force—it was a real orgy of extremism. The functioning of the Supreme Soviet [in Azerbaijan] had been paralyzed and the deputies subjected to blackmail. In that situation certain specially authorized bodies—the President's Council, represented by its member Primakov [who later became foreign minister and prime minister under Yeltsin] and the CPSU Central Committee Secretary Girenko—reported that the Supreme Soviet in the Azerbaijan Republic was unable to perform its functions and that emergency measures were required to reestablish constitutional order and prevent still greater bloodshed. The central government of the Soviet Union at that time took the measure of declaring a state of emergency in Baku. But it's well known that peace did not come to the land of Azerbaijan as a result.

As for the events in Tbilisi and Vilnius, what happened there took place without my participation. What was involved was a political provocation aimed at discrediting the policies of perestroika and the president of the USSR himself in the eyes of the local population and abroad.

In the dramatic situation that existed in 1991 I placed my bets on political methods of solving problems by hastening preparations for the signing of the Union Treaty, the adoption of a new party program, and the elaboration of a program to deal with the crisis. But when this had been achieved the August coup followed, knocking our country off the road of evolutionary reform.

z.m. Not only do I remember that, Misha, but I had my own point of view at the time, which I shared with you in June 1991 for the last time. I also knew that the developing situation was full of contradictions. I was convinced that your negative attitude in principle toward the use of force was correct, and I wrote about that several times and spoke publicly about it both before August 1991 and after that. Moreover, I explained your desire to concentrate as many powers as possible in your own hands as coming from your wish to prevent someone else from resorting to the use of force without your permission or against your will. However, on the basis of several political discussions in Moscow and judging from the general atmosphere in the party apparatus and government apparatus, I did feel that plans for a coup were in the air. However, I thought it necessary that you, as the embodiment of supreme governmental and party authority, should clearly demonstrate that you did hold power in your hands, that that's where the real power and authority were, not somewhere else. Because at that time it seemed to me there were two things that were almost equally important: not only not to allow oneself to be provoked into the use of force but also not to let the authority of the central government be lost in the eyes of the people. When people stop believing that their highest leader holds real power, then in reality he has already lost half the game. But I also did not see any specific and clearly effective way out of the existing situation.

Power That Is Not Used Loses Its Authority

M.G.   I consider the choice I made in that complicated time to be correct. First, the opponents of perestroika did not succeed in pushing me out of the picture or driving me into a corner. They wanted to establish a blood bond with me, to subordinate me to a kind of gangsters' mutual protection society, a situation in which a person is left with nowhere to turn. They wanted to confront me with an accomplished fact, but they did not succeed in doing anything like that. They tried to have me removed from the post I held; they tried this at plenary sessions of the Central Committee, Congresses of People's Deputies, and sessions of the Supreme Soviet. But their plans were frustrated, and moreover this was done by political means. Second, I invariably received the support of the USSR Supreme Soviet and the union republics, which was an expression and a result of my actual influence as president of the country.

Z.M.   But in the end the republics succeeded in dissolving the Soviet Union.

M.G.   You can't say that. The disintegration of the country occurred as the result of the adventuristic coup of August 1991 and the very crude mistakes of the Russian leadership, which had charted a course toward the destruction of the Soviet Union.

Z.M.   Yes, today you have every right to say the following three things: I never yielded to those who wanted to crush the union republics, never agreed to a policy that would have led to a catastrophic impoverishment and other social consequences, and on the international arena the USSR remained one of the most important forces determining the main direction of world politics.

M.G.   Not only can I say this about myself, but many others also see it now who did not want to see it at the time. Testifying to this are many letters I have received, whose quantity has significantly increased since the events of October 1993 [Yeltsin's bombardment and suppression of the Russian Supreme Soviet]. A few days ago someone called me from Peredelkino [a Moscow suburb where many prominent individuals have country homes, or dachas]. Several well-known writers had gathered at a dacha. Some of them had supported the conservative forces opposed to perestroika but now had decided they wanted to talk with me. Some of them asked me to forgive them for verbal assaults they had made against me. And the general trend of the conversation was quite unambiguous: "We tried to undermine you, but today we see that you were right in regard to both economic reform and the reshaping of the Soviet federation."

z.m.   Of course you can take satisfaction in that, coming after long delay, but that should not divert us from the original question. Don't you think that sometimes you should have used your power more swiftly, more resolutely, and more broadly to weaken the forces that in the end resorted to the coup? Couldn't you have used your power to strengthen your own centrist position relative to the radicals on both sides?

m.g.   After the August coup, Zdeněk, I had to listen to so much harsh criticism, partly just and partly unjust, that I could no longer leave this question unanswered. Even then, at a session of the USSR Supreme Soviet, I said that I felt and accepted my responsibility for the fact that as president I had not done everything necessary to prevent a coup, not to allow one to happen. Evidently I should have taken more care to create guarantees against such a danger, in order not only to weaken the positions of the *nomenklatura* but also to establish effective mechanisms that would have ruled out the possibility of the army and security agencies being used to carry out such actions without the consent of the Supreme Soviet, etc. Looking back, we can ask the question: Wasn't it possible to change the situation for the better—in general, as well as by means of certain specific measures? One thing I can say: there was no simple recipe, nothing I had failed to observe, that would have improved the situation through the use of force. The main thing that made it impossible for a coup to turn the country back to pre-perestroika conditions was the new social and political atmosphere in the country and the new international situation, which had been freed of the worst forms of Cold War confrontation. All of that was achieved by carrying out the policies of perestroika.

z.m.   All that is true, and I myself have written on several occasions that one of your greatest services to the development of a democratic political culture in Russia remains that you did not resort to force when the developing process of events in your country ceased to correspond to your conceptions. That you, so to speak, subordinated your desire for political success and the preservation of your power to the general principles and values of democracy. I also agree that it was not possible to "preserve socialism" solely by intervening with power. At the same time I think that for historians a question will remain: Wasn't it possible at a certain moment, not just in 1990, but much earlier, by a more decisive use of concentrated power to influence events and perhaps prevent the course of development that began after the August coup?

All this reminds me, Misha, of a question that I myself was tormented by after 1968, a question which, to this day, historians have answered in different ways. (And probably things will stay that way.) The question is: Would it not have been possible during the Prague Spring to have given more consideration to the possibility of Soviet intervention, to have tried to prevent it by following a more cautious policy? Later, after many experiences and after reflecting on this for a long time, I came to a conclusion that I still hold to this day—namely, that we could have avoided Soviet intervention if in general we had not tried to change the system fundamentally but had restricted ourselves to some sort of cosmetic operations. Then most likely there would not have been August 1968, but there also would not have been the Prague Spring. But for historians, as I have said, this question remains open. They will continue in the future to debate over whether things could have been different, the question of "what if?" . . .

There's Only One World

1. BREAKING OUT OF THE DEAD END OF THE COLD WAR

Z.M.   Everything that we have said so far can actually be stated, from the point of view of our conception of socialism, in the following sentence: On the basis of our own experience we ceased to identify socialism with a system of the Soviet type, and from this we gradually arrived at the conviction that socialism cannot be understood as an isolated "anticapitalist formation" existing apart in one or several countries. In other words, the so-called socialist camp did not have some sort of exclusive proprietary rights to socialism; on the other hand, it could not be said that the so-called capitalist camp was an area that had nothing socialist about it. Consequently the conflict between two camps could not be equated with the struggle for socialism (or the struggle against it). What the ideologists depicted as the chief form of the working class struggle against capital throughout the world in actuality had degenerated into a power-politics military conflict between two different great-power blocs.

I myself came to this conclusion rather quickly under the impact of Soviet military intervention in 1968, although as I have already described in detail, during the Prague Spring I considered the so-called socialist camp itself to be, if not the only, certainly the decisive factor in the development and revitalization of socialism. After my arrival in the West in 1977, I quickly came to the realization that the concept of "two camps," two rival military-political blocs, had nothing original about it. It was also present in left-wing circles, particularly in the peace movement and the environmentalist movement. Despite all the positive things that the policy of détente brought with it, in contrast to the classic Cold War period of the 1950s, the negative logic of this conflict remained the basis for the prevailing ideology and politics. Each bloc regarded its own military power as the chief factor preventing war and assuring peace. Because of this the rivalry in the arms race could never be ended; it could only be regulated. Within the framework of "peaceful coexistence" and "détente," there continued to exist an oversimplified division of the world into two rival camps, subordination of all other processes to the interests of the two blocs, and ideas to the effect that although no one really wanted a war, nevertheless in the final analysis it would have to be seen who would defeat whom. Finally, the very concept of détente, or relaxation of tensions, was based on the presumption that tensions in fact continued to exist, and that no one knew how to remove them.

There were only a few small democratic movements and individual intellectuals who proposed that both the tension in the world and its causes could be removed on the basis of a new understanding of the contemporary world and its global problems, the concept of general human interests and values. None of those who argued along such lines was a representative of any government that might even have begun to try to put such ideas into practice—against the policies of the great powers. All of this changed fundamentally when Gorbachev appeared with the new thinking and gradually began to demonstrate that, rather than just a new type of propaganda or ideology, this was a concept of politics that really could be put into practice by one of the two superpowers in the world.

To me, Misha, all this was logically connected with your conception of a fundamental reform of the Soviet system. But many people thought that the attempt to revitalize socialism and a policy that would transcend existing blocs, including the Soviet bloc—that for you those were two different things. Was that so? Or was the idea of overcoming the division of the world into two competing blocs actually one of the conditions for the revitalization of socialism? By the way, to this day an idea is being bruited about, and often successfully, that the West, by imposing the arms race on the USSR, forced it to change its foreign policy. It turns out, according to this argument, that the main source of Gorbachev's new thinking was Reagan's old thinking.

The Danger Was That We Would All Go to Hell in the Same Basket

M.G.   I would say that the decisive thing was the desire of the reformers to fundamentally change the domestic situation in the USSR to overcome stagnation, to achieve a new kind of dynamic in development, to allow the possibilities inherent in socialism, as we put it then—to allow them to unfold, to rejuvenate socialism. An essential component of this orientation was to have a new conception of the world.

That meant the recognition that there exists a single interconnected and interdependent world. A world that is complex and full of contradictions, but is nevertheless a single, inseparable whole. For that reason the problems of one "camp" cannot be resolved without considering the other "camp" and its problems. Instead of just existing side by side, it's necessary to arrive at some sort of mutual cooperation and collaboration between different economic and sociopolitical systems. But cooperation, and ultimately partnership, could not push conflict out of the way as long as the division of the world into opposing military-political blocs existed. The roots of the new thinking lay in the understanding that there would be no winners in a nuclear war and that in any such event both "camps" would be blown to kingdom come.

We recognized diversity and alternative paths of development and, consequently, the possibility of various choices that could not be imposed by force. We considered this the beginning of a new, open process of development in the world, one that would not have the character of an instantaneous leap or explosion, but of gradual, long-term change. As I have said, in the West they thought this didn't concern them, that it was just a matter of the collapse of Communism. Today political forces in the West are beginning to understand that the problems of the development of the whole modern world do affect the Western countries in full measure.

The Cold War Was a Dead End

Z.M.   Some in the West recognize this, but others are still strutting around claiming that the West "won the Cold War." In this they are pursuing two goals: one, to justify the Cold War in retrospect; and two, to give what would seem to be a definitive answer to every question. They are saying that only the ideologists on the Western front of the Cold War were right and remain so. They try to make things look as though history has ended with Radio Liberty and Radio Free Europe defeating the ideological departments of the CPSU Central Committee and the other Communist parties. It might be possible to dismiss all this as something laughable and unworthy of attention, had not such "reasoning" become a definite political force in the countries where "actually existing socialism" once held sway. Even today in those countries this kind of oversimplified view of the world, still entangled in Cold War logic, supports the illusion that all one has to do is copy "Western" models as quickly as possible and as exactly as possible, and then a society of the Soviet type will immediately be transformed into a society of the Western type, with a high standard of living and a functioning pluralistic democracy. The disillusionment that is bound to set in after the collapse of such illusory concepts will inevitably hurt the development of democracy and help populist demagogues.

M.G.   The oversimplified idea that the West "won the Cold War" began to spread especially in the years 1989–1992. This idea persists above all because of support for it by an odd alliance between Western conservative ideologists and local conservatives in our country and in other countries of the former Soviet bloc. The former are simply puffed up with braggadocio, and our conservatives locally support their viewpoint as alleged proof that the reformers here "betrayed" both socialism and our homeland, along with its national interests. I would describe such a conception as mere political game playing.

The effectiveness of this approach is gradually weakening, above all in the West itself, where many people are already capable of seeing realistically what difficult and burdensome problems this so-called victory has brought them. In my recent trips to many different countries I became convinced that not only among intellectuals but also in political and business circles more and more people who understand this are making their appearance. To ask the question "Who won the Cold

War?" is not only unscientific; it is not even serious. There were no winners; rather, everybody lost . . .

Z.M.   Because it was a dead end in which we were stuck for many long years, and we all paid an unimaginably high price for it.

M.G.   Yes, that's exactly right. Taking the USSR and USA alone, about 10 trillion dollars was burned up in the furnace of the arms race in each of these countries. But the initiative for finding a way out of the dead end was taken, after all, only with the new thinking in Soviet policy. Today we see the growth of an ever greater understanding of the necessity for a new paradigm of world civilization, one that would transcend the old concepts of socialism and capitalism as hostile social formations.

Z.M.   In the interests of objectivity and a fair evaluation of things one point should be added to this—namely, that in the conflict between value orientations predominating, on the one hand, in the open society of the West and, on the other, in the totalitarian systems of the Soviet type, the defeat of the latter is an indisputable fact.

M.G.   I remember that during talks on the island of Malta with President George Bush and Secretary of State James Baker in December 1989 a discussion suddenly started up over whether it is possible to talk about "Western values" as the basis for the new course of development in the world. I said at the time that for me the main thing was the openness of different kinds of societies in relation to one another and not scholastic ideological disputes that threaten to become some sort of new "holy war." We agreed that a positive process of development was possible on the basis of "democratic values." I agreed with this because the end of the Cold War can be viewed, from this angle, not as the victory of one side over another in an ideological conflict but as the transcending of this whole vicious cycle.

Z.M.   Throughout history such changes have usually occurred under compulsion. Not because of the strength of armies but under the pressure of new historical circumstances. So far only the system of the Soviet type has been affected, and therefore the onset of a new phase in the development of civilization can for the time being be interpreted in an oversimplified way to mean merely the defeat of socialism.

Overcoming the Legacy of the Cold War

M.G.   I think that in this case, too, one must admit that the concept of the defeat of socialism is incorrect. Significant changes are also occurring in the so-called victorious countries and much more will have to change in them in the future. The West needs a kind of perestroika of its own. We have always emphasized that the new thinking is necessary both for us and for the whole world, and as time goes by this will enter into the consciousness of Western politicians, although not so quickly or so easily.

Z.M.   In connection with this, Misha, I have sometimes had the impression that you perhaps are inclined to overestimate the desire and will among ruling circles in the West to support your understanding of things, whereas your counterparts in fact have always pursued their own interests. It was none other than you, on your first trip to London as early as 1984, who publicly quoted Disraeli, I think, to the effect that Britain has no permanent friends or permanent enemies; it only has permanent interests . . .

M.G.   It was Palmerston who said that.

Z.M.   All right. But still, I haven't got the meaning of the quotation wrong, and it's appropriate to today's international politics as well. I'm definitely not one of those who denounced your initiative in ending the Cold War as a betrayal of the cause of socialism and of Russia. As for the role of the national interests of various governments, however, I understood as early as 1968 that the Western governments, which had their own worries about the student movements in Paris and in Germany at the time, were not going to interfere too much when Communism showed the world its tanks instead of a "human face."

I sometimes feared that you were too trusting in regard to the intentions of the Western governments, as far as their giving any genuine support to the revitalization of socialism.

I followed closely what you were saying in your speeches, and I know that they were always carefully weighed and thought out. You spoke especially clearly about all this in your Nobel Prize lecture in Oslo in 1991. I regard that as a concise and sincere explanation of your political convictions; you stated quite clearly what needs to be done and what had already been done by the USSR. And you also said that Western policymakers now had their turn. You did not conceal the fact that if the West failed to give effective help to the whole process of fundamental change in the world, then the entire process would be in jeopardy. I think that the West then took a wait-and-see attitude, calculating what would be in its interests and what would not. And we still encounter the same thing today.

M.G.   Of course neither then nor now was I so naïve as to think that the West would help reform "socialism." But we had to develop our own initiative aimed at ending the Cold War because without that it would have been impossible to take the decisive steps of perestroika. This was both for economic reasons, primarily those connected with demilitarization of the economy, and for basic ideological and political reasons, mainly connected with the principle of freedom of choice within the Soviet bloc and within the USSR itself.

And of course in my reflections I never went so far as to suppose that people, either in the West or in the socialist countries, would renounce the advancement of their own interests or the demand that those interests be satisfied. No, I never did that, but I saw as the quintessence of the new thinking the recognition of freedom of choice and the necessity for a balance of interests. More than that, there was not one unified position in the West on the changes in the USSR. I remember on one occasion, at a meeting with Western foreign ministers, a discussion started up about the reforms in our country. This was in

September 1990. It turned out that the Americans, the French, and the Germans had quite different views regarding the question of a choice of systems.

Nevertheless the West did have one clear common interest: that the USSR should become a democratic state which recognized the common rules of the game like all other states. That did not mean that the West wanted this to happen within the framework of the socialist choice. That of course was not in the interests of the West. Many in the West were not pleased, also, by the fact that fundamental changes in the world were taking place as a result of Soviet initiative. Especially that this initiative was coming from the general secretary of the Communist Party. Still, this was understandable to me because they were of course proceeding from their own interests. Nevertheless, gradually the positions of Western leaders shifted, and more and more often you could hear acknowledgments that each country must have freedom of choice and that it is necessary to take into account the interests not only of the great powers but of the smaller powers as well.

z.m.   But what is happening now is something different, a kind of return to the old way of viewing things.

m.g.   Yes, but I think that in the West there will gradually come to prevail an understanding that precisely in its own interest a change of views on the new problems of worldwide development must be made. That the ruins of the Cold War are not a good foundation for building the future. But all this could serve as the basis for a separate discussion, and let's return to this subject later on.

z.m.   I did want to say something on this particular subject: it is possible that before an approach that corresponds to the new situation in the world begins to be applied to practical politics in the West—it's possible that surviving remnants of the Cold War outlook in the East will become stronger. All this is because, with the end of the Cold War, although the so-called socialist camp itself has disappeared, still another kind of camp has remained, and it is only slowly changing its outlook on things. The result is that those people who never stopped conceiving of socialism in the old way, as an "anticapitalist system in a separate country" or in a "separate bloc of countries," both those people and people who measure the greatness of Russia primarily by its ability to be a force in the world in military respects equal to the United States and NATO, these people are also, strictly speaking, returning to the logic of the Cold War.

M.G.   But from this very fact there flows a quite definite conclusion, that it is impermissible to forget about the new thinking; more than that, it is necessary to develop the new thinking further, because that is the only way to take advantage of the opportunities that have been opened by our extricating ourselves from the Cold War. The logical result of acknowledging the interconnection and interdependency of the world should, after all, be the recognition that general human values and needs must take precedence over class conflicts; also, the viewpoint that violence is the driving force in history must be renounced. Our experience of introducing the principles of the new thinking into Soviet foreign policy shows that this is not an easy thing to do: rising up against our efforts were not only old habits of thought but also real social forces linked by material interests with the old way of doing things—from the generals and other high-ranking officers to the scientists, all of whom had made their careers on the basis of "demonstrating" the irreconcilable nature of the "two camps in the world." For that very reason I can imagine that in the West, too, it is a matter of a difficult and prolonged process. But not only is it possible there as well; it is absolutely necessary. There is a risk that history will not give us enough time for the new thinking to truly win out worldwide. Of course that danger exists, but still there is simply no other choice. There are things that are stronger and more powerful than the calculations of the present moment, the seeking of current advantage. I have in mind the global challenges whose impact is bound to grow.

Z.M.   I would like at this point to return to where we began: to the fact that the so-called socialist camp disappeared together with the

Cold War, but that does not mean that socialism disappeared from the world. The only people who see things in that way are those for whom socialism exists only when a so-called socialist system predominates in a particular country. From this point of view, socialism today is reduced to China and a few small countries. I personally do not deny that such a conception of socialism may in some parts of the world still operate as a genuine political force, particularly in certain developing countries of Asia and Latin America. But for the long-term perspectives of socialism, both in the West and in the countries of the former Soviet bloc, I see no solution in that kind of conception. On this we are in agreement, and the question on the agenda now, switching over to a new subject for our conversation, is this:

What is our conception of socialism after the Cold War and the disappearance of the so-called socialist camp?

2. SOCIALISM IS ALIVE AS A WORLD PROCESS

z.m. Official Soviet ideology for many long years proclaimed that socialism exists only where certain general so-called laws of socialism are embodied in practice: public (or state) property in the decisive means of production, collective property in agriculture, economic planning obligatory for developing the economy, the leading role of the Communist Party (and through it, of the working class), and socialist internationalism, which in practice meant obligatory adherence to orders from Moscow for all other Communist parties.

From the course of our conversation it has become quite unambiguously clear that each of us, in different ways and at different times, but ultimately in a thoroughgoing way on both of our parts, rejected these so-called universal laws as criteria for socialism, but we did accept these as indications in general of the characteristics possessed by systems of Stalinist origin. These were very precisely and concisely formulated attributes of totalitarian government power, a system of total control over all of the life of society, which on an international scale was subordinated to a single center in Moscow. In our view, these attributes stand in contradiction to genuine socialism because they exclude democracy. All of this, however, is merely a statement of what socialism is not in our understanding. We need to give a positive answer to the question: What do we actually consider socialism to be? But in order to do that, it would be best to start with another question:

Was Soviet Society Socialist?

M.G. I think that I've partly answered this question already. I only want to add that to the extent that I came to the conclusion, over the course of time, that perestroika would necessarily have to mean the change of the entire system, to that extent I kept coming closer to a negative answer to the question, Was the system that prevailed in the USSR socialism? Soviet society was a totalitarian system, with all the consequences that followed from that for its citizens.

Z.M. Nevertheless it was not capitalism . . .

In my opinion, societies of the Soviet type represented in principle a noncapitalist form of industrial civilization that displayed, along with certain socialist elements, which were usually distorted and deformed in all kinds of ways, some quite remarkable pre-capitalist elements and relations.

This was expressed particularly in the attitude of political power toward society as a whole, toward its groups and toward the individual, as well as in the relation between political power and the economy. The political authorities tried to take upon themselves the role of the market. They tried to determine, through economic planning, what, where, when, how, and for whom goods would be produced without any regard for increasing the amount of capital, that is, profits.

The political power was always the only active agency, the direct participant in decisive economic and social relations. That was what gave it the possibility of "directing the life of society," in fact subordinating the life of society to its totalitarian control. Although it was not capitalist, it was also not socialist, but antidemocratic. It did not in any way lead to the greater emancipation of human beings; on the contrary, it reduced their freedom, and resulted in less emancipation than in the contemporary society of the Western type, which had grown up on the basis of capitalist economic relations. It follows from this, however, that even from the socialist viewpoint, not everything anti-capitalist is good, and not everything capitalist is bad. So within the framework of this many-sided set of interconnected considerations, I agree with your view that the totalitarian system of political power was decisive for the character of Soviet society.

The Soviet system did have a certain relation to socialism on the ideological plane. This was its relation to Marxist socialist thought. Lenin's conceptions, above all on the question of the dictatorship of the proletariat and the role of the revolutionary vanguard party, in practice actually did become one of the sources of the totalitarian system of the Soviet type. This cannot be denied, but one cannot fail to see that Bolshevik ideology was only one factor in the rise of this system. The totalitarian system did not originate in the October revolution of 1917, but developed in the post-revolutionary decades.

In the process a decisive role, in my opinion, was played by factors that were not at all socialist, but simply historical, and they in turn affected the understanding of socialism in Soviet ideology. I personally attribute fundamental importance to five of these factors. The first is the historic circumstance that Russia had not gone through the phase of development that Western European capitalism had in the nineteenth and early twentieth centuries. Therefore it lacked a developed social structure of civil society and the forms of democratic political culture growing out of that. A second factor is the state of war that the Soviet system encountered during various phases of its existence, from World War I, through the Russian Civil War, to World War II and the Cold War; and under wartime conditions the totalitarian form of power had certain advantages. A third factor was the world economic crisis of capitalism in the 1930s, accompanied by a crisis of political democracy and the onset of totalitarian dictatorships of the Nazi and Fascist type in Europe. The sharpening social conflicts, and the use of force connected with them, up to and including terrorism as a method of rule, were, strictly speaking, part of the spirit of the times.

A fourth factor was the isolation of the Soviet system from the rest of the world—first, as a result of Western blockade, later as a result of the Stalinist conception of "socialism in a single country." Later this isolation was maintained under a new form, "the world socialist camp." But the importance of that fourth factor only increased in connection with the fifth factor, which I regard as the victory of the USSR in World War II. A system that had been victorious in the biggest war the world had ever seen, that had brought a significant part of the world under its rule, the system that prevailed within the borders of one of the great superpowers of the world—that kind of system was able to reject criticism for many long years and reject the need for any fundamental changes, but it was able to reject such things only superficially; on a deeper level such rejection had disastrous consequences for the system itself. Although the Soviet system, then, was not the embodiment of the socialist idea, for many decades it equated itself with socialism or was identified with socialism both by its own supporters and by a significant majority of its opponents.

This was possible not only because it called itself socialism, but also because there were some elements of socialism in the society living under this system. As supporters of the socialist idea, even today we must openly acknowledge this fact: that is, we cannot simply proclaim that since it was not socialism, it is only a frightening example of how not to try to carry out the idea of socialism. Looking back, Misha, don't you also see socialist elements within Soviet society? Didn't the collapse of the Soviet system also involve the loss of certain valuable elements from the point of view of socialist values?

Entire Generations Lived and Fought—and Not in Vain

M.G. It may come as a surprise to you, but among the positive values that have been lost I put in first place the fact that people then did believe in socialism. The impulse provided by the revolution had a powerful effect: freedom, land, and the factories to those who worked them, human dignity for those who had been humiliated—the belief in all those values was, in spite of everything, something quite positive.

These were socialist, but at the same time simply humanist and eman-
cipatory aspirations. And people believed that they should accept sacrifices and endure hardships in order to open the road for the realization of these aspirations. In the last few decades this impulse ceased to
operate so strongly; instead, there was a growing sense among the
people that we had lost our original goals. But I think that for a very
long time the belief in those values, and the hope for their realization,
was practical proof that the people, in spite of all the difficulties and
horrors that we experienced since 1917, and there were a countless
number of them, the people never stopped searching for a way forward
to a more just social system.

Of course all this would have been impossible if people had perceived and experienced Soviet society only as a system imposed by
force that did not give them anything positive. For many years people
experienced an extraordinarily high rate of industrial growth, the tan-
gible and undeniable change from a backward country into an indus-
trialized country. People came from remote villages to work in new
factories, which they took pride in as their own accomplishment in a
sincere and genuine manner. The eradication of illiteracy, access to
education, and visible improvement in living conditions for the masses
after ominous destruction and starvation—all this was not just propaganda, but people's actual experience. After the victory in World
War II people once again saw that without industrialization we would
have lost to the Nazi armies. There existed a truly positive subjective
attitude toward Soviet society on the part of entire generations who
connected their dearest hopes and plans in life with the success of that
society. Socialist goals were an ideal and an object of orientation for
many individual human lives, and this cannot be overlooked or simply
thrown out or rejected when we evaluate our past. All this does not
mean that the Soviet system was socialist, but for a long time within
Soviet society these kinds of values were operative, and they were quite
positive from the point of view of socialism.

z.m.   After all, belief in certain values can be the first step toward
making them a reality. True, this may not come about, but without

that belief no step in a definite direction can be taken. This can also be extended to religious beliefs and to various kinds of civilizing impulses or aspirations.

M.G.   Yes, and we ourselves right here and now are conducting a conversation about the contradictory past that began at one point with our belief in Communism, without which the chronicle of our lives would have been quite different. This was far from merely being faith in human emancipation. That kind of faith is not included in the presently fashionable image of that society as one lacking in any contradictions, a time of "total darkness." After all, can the enormous work done in the fields of education and science be simply thrown out? Why, education and health care are the basis of any system of social justice. Only when people have equal access to education, regardless of their social status, can they be called on to develop their talents and find their place in society on the basis of their abilities.

Finally, even if we condemn whatever deserves to be condemned, we cannot deny the existence within Soviet society of a desire for social justice. This is a very complex set of problems, full of contradictions, because tendencies moving in opposite directions were operating simultaneously. On the one hand, there were the privileges of the *nomenklatura* and the dishonest ways in which some groups and individuals enriched themselves, and on the other hand, there were the quite harmful tendencies toward "leveling," but I will leave all that aside for now. On the whole it can be said that in the provision of the basic needs of life there was not a profound polarization among different social groups. Even at the lowest levels of the social ladder people did not live in such hopeless circumstances that lack of social mobility was transferred from generation to generation, as is typical for those living in poverty in many countries with capitalist economies.

Z.M.   The situation in that respect brings China to mind. When I first traveled there in 1981 it was quite evident that it was a developing country with a very low standard of living for the masses. However, the poverty there did not leap out at you like the horrible misery and despair of the slums so common to the Third World countries with capitalist economies.

M.G.   Yes, in evaluating Soviet society, it's possible to speak of a barracks type of socialism based on shortages or an insufficient standard of living. But there was a system of social protection, and support was provided for people's social needs. All of that existed, of course, within the framework of a low material standard of living, a barracks-type regimentation. Incidentally, the experience of social support provided for people in Soviet society had an influence on the development of the modern welfare state in general.

Z.M.   I would say even more. Soviet society was for many decades— both before and after World War II—a most important source of pressure on capitalism in the interests of people who live by wage labor. The postwar "welfare state" in the West and the retreat from the traditional methods of capitalism throughout the world—this would hardly have happened without the "Soviet threat" to the indestructible reign of capital. It was not a military threat, but a social one. Even in its regimented "barracks" form, that system of greater social equality was a force to be reckoned with.

M.G.   Equality of poverty is not of course a socialist ideal or goal. But even at the stage of development in Soviet society when equality had that aspect, an important principle was affirmed—that the minimal needs of life should be guaranteed by the government and by society for all individuals. The very principle of these social guarantees has to do with the right to life, or the right to a decent life, and it corresponds to the interests of freedom, liberty, and the emancipation of humanity; it is a socialist value and a general humanist value. As a principle it does not stand in contradiction to the acceptance of inequality in material possessions. This principle does not exclude a certain kind of inequality in general. The principle of social guarantees comes into effect when there is a danger that poverty will undermine a person's existence, when it is a threat to people's lives and the lives of their children.

Z.M.   Yes. Besides that, it can't be forgotten that the tendency toward such equality within the framework of poverty was a feature of other nonsocialist movements, in particular, early Christianity.

M.G.   When society as a whole provides guarantees to all its members, or to those of its members who are threatened by catastrophe, then properly speaking it is only a form of human solidarity. And solidarity, in turn, is a value that is not only socialist. It is also linked with the idea of collectivism, but they are not identical things. In practice solidarity manifests itself more easily in a state of poverty or need, when people obviously feel a common danger, but from that you can't conclude that when there is prosperity and plenty, solidarity becomes irrelevant. Why, even Hobbes knew that without solidarity the principle of "dog eat dog" would prevail and that no community can live on the basis of such a principle, but that there would only be a hidden war of each against all.

The denial of solidarity, the deliberate flouting of this principle, which we see in Russia today, represents a loss not only for socialism but also for humanism in general. The rise of narrow self-seeking and the decline of solidarity are processes that have been taking place in our country for a long time now; they were especially evident during the Brezhnev era of stagnation. After the dissolution of the USSR this developed into an ideology enjoying government blessing.

The feeling of solidarity in Soviet society was extended, of course, both to the poor and the oppressed beyond the borders of the USSR, especially in the Third World. I'm convinced that the government could not have supported anti-colonial movements on such a large scale if the Soviet people had not felt an obligation to help those movements.

If I were to summarize how I view Soviet society, I could say approximately the following: from the historical point of view it was a dead end in social development, but within that society many things had come into existence that were positive for people even then, and that have meaning for the future. So then, our grandfathers and fathers did not live in vain.

The Conception of Socialism from the Point of View of Values

z.m.   Although we do not identify or equate the Soviet system with socialism, we do share the opinion that this type of society had socialist elements, that a socialist tendency was operative within it.

The decisive role in Soviet society was played, however, not by the socialist elements, but by the totalitarian structure of power. The appearance of capitalist tendencies on the scene in the so-called post-Communist countries is the inevitable result of the disintegration of that power structure, and thus there has become evident in these societies something that previously was concealed by ideology—namely, that socialist elements and tendencies were and are only one of the factors at work there. But the same thing can be observed throughout the modern world. Socialist elements and tendencies existed not only in Soviet society but also—to varying degrees in different walks of life—in societies where the decisive role is played by capitalist tendencies. What has collapsed above all is the false conception that the contradiction between socialist and capitalist tendencies is embodied in the contradiction between the "two opposing camps in the world," the notion that each camp supposedly embodied only one tendency.

m.g.   Back then, Zdeněk, what that meant was that all our previous notions of socialism and capitalism had to be changed. To acknowledge that we would never find "pure socialism" also meant to understand that no "pure capitalism" had ever existed, either in the past or at the beginning of the twentieth century. I will not be telling you much that's new when I tell you about the conclusions I drew from that. I've already spoken of this before, in concise and summary form, for example, at the congress of the Socialist International in Berlin in the fall of 1992. For myself I have renounced a deterministic scheme of things as put forward by the Soviet school of so-called Marxism. I see that it was wrong from the start to regard socialism as a special formation that represents something historically inevitable in the development of humankind. My whole experience has convinced me that a value-based conception of socialism is more correct. It is a process in which people seek to realize certain values, and in this process all progressive and democratic ideas and practical experiences are integrated.

z.m.   On the whole I agree with that. Whereas you and I arrived at such a conclusion by different paths, and whereas this was a discovery of fundamental importance and a turning point for both of us, on the other hand, this kind of conception of socialism had already been tested by experience in one place or another, with results that have always, of course, been both positive and negative. Arguments and disputes are going on now and will continue in regard to a value-based conception of socialism.

m.g.   The worst thing of all is when some movement or party pretends to have the only correct solution.

But let me return to what I had begun to say. I consider the main socialist values—in accordance with all democratic socialist tendencies—above all to be freedom, equality, justice, and solidarity. These are the values that have been preached by entire generations who fought for freedom and dignity for working people, for the oppressed and exploited, and under the banner of these values huge mass movements have arisen. Although in Russia today, and in some other places, the very concept of socialism is rejected, while crude and primitive attacks against socialism have become the fashion, nevertheless more and more people are asking themselves disturbing questions: What will the future bring? Where are we headed? I think that—maybe not today, so soon after the fall of the Soviet system, but after a certain length of time, when we will have lived through a new experience—an acceptable answer to such questions for a significant part of society will be precisely those values linked with the socialist idea.

In our era, however, all ideological conceptions of the future will be compared on the basis of how they understand and deal with global problems, how they correspond to the general interests of humanity.

Conceptions that proceed mainly from the needs of particular classes or individual nations will also be measured against those general problems and interests. If they remain closed within themselves instead of providing answers to global challenges, it seems to me they will not serve as a starting point for a new conceptual view of the future. The socialist idea, however, can become such a starting point since the basic values connected with it have a universal character. It is true that the idea of socialism should be separated from a concept of social interests mainly based on adherence to a group. From an ideology that at one time was solely based on class we should create a "meta-ideology," enabling a constantly increasing number of people to find a common language. The socialist idea, thus, could become global humanism.

z.m.   I understand the direction of your thinking, Misha, and your intention seems to me correct, and yet I must ask: What constitutes the special quality of precisely socialist values in this case? You yourself have already said or written in one place or another that the idea of socialism is as old as the eternal hopes of humanity, that Christianity was actually the beginning of the socialist idea, and that it cannot disappear because people will always strive for freedom and a just social system. This line of argument is true, but also not true: the socialist idea, although it seeks for a way to make a reality of these ancient ideas, nevertheless has only sought to do so in the modern era, essentially with the rise of capitalism, in opposition to it, and in close association with the working class movement.

It is true that the classical proletariat of an earlier day and its class-based movement no longer exist today, at least not in the advanced Western countries, and thus the idea of socialism cannot base itself on the interests of nonexistent class forces. But I don't think you can prove from this that the socialist idea has ceased to be linked with a search for a way to make a reality of the values linked with socialism precisely in industrial society, or so-called postindustrial society, where the decisive dynamic continues to be the expansion of capital. Therefore the socialist idea cannot consist only in the advocacy of certain values; it must also answer the question of how to put them into practice in spite of opposing tendencies, especially capitalist tendencies, that seek to subordinate people everywhere to the laws of the market and the interests of profit. It is worthwhile for us to move onto new ground, to ask what practical efforts are to be made for advancing socialist values. And we cannot avoid the question: Which social relations and institutions serve as aids to those values, and which ones, on the contrary, serve to hinder the implementation of those values? Here we are stepping onto thin ice, because as soon as the problem of social relations and institutions comes up—whether we wish it or not—we find ourselves in spite of everything in the realm of property relations, institutions of political power, forms of democracy, and so on.

M.G. In connection with the discussion of the subject "freedom of choice" you said in one of your comments earlier that, strictly speaking, I was advocating liberalism, which is insufficient for socialism. I commented that we could have a discussion about that later on, and this is the appropriate moment to do that.

Of course we cannot go into a history of the development of liberal or socialist thought here. I will therefore talk only about the contemporary or current state of affairs concerning this problem. Since the downfall of the Soviet system a number of attempts have been made to portray this as the total victory of liberalism in its contemporary neoliberal political form. Things have gone as far as the assertion that "the end of history" has been reached. I agree with your criticism on this point. But I do wish to single out another aspect of the whole problem. It's well known that long before the Soviet system reached its end, even before it came into existence, liberalism was forced in practice, under the pressure of the socialist movement, to retreat from its principles in many respects: its defense of economic efficiency against social justice, and of the free market against regulatory intervention by the state. At the same time socialists who were operating in parliamentary democracies were forced to accept and in practice adopt certain political measures originated by liberalism, because otherwise they could not have stayed in power.

In reality, only as a result of these mutual compromises has both

the effective regulation of crisis situations and the maintenance of social peace and a high standard of living for most people in the advanced
Western countries been possible, and indirectly this has led to the practical success of the scientific and technological revolution. Isn't this a
convincing argument against sharply counterposing liberalism and socialism? At the same time, of course, it remains a fact that liberal democracy has not solved important problems of the economic and social
emancipation of wage labor. On the other hand, when the socialist
concept that the working class can be elevated to freedom through the
"dictatorship of the proletariat" was turned into an absolute rule, this
led in practice to totalitarian regimes. Isn't this an argument against
the idea that only one or another ideological tendency is the exclusive
possessor of the only "correct solution"? The socialist idea is a search
and an exploration. It may be only a contribution to a general process
of exploration of various paths of development in the contemporary
world. Genuinely historical ways of solving problems on the level of
entire civilizations generally transcend the framework of ideologies;
they lie on the other side of ideology.

Socialist Relations and Institutions

z.m.   I agree, Misha. But I insist that we have stepped onto the thin
ice of the problem of property relations and democratic institutions.
After all, even your arguments about fruitful compromise between liberalism and socialism indicate that the outcome of the debate over
various values and orientations must be embodied in quite definite
social relations and institutions. What is your understanding of socialism on this level?

m.g.   Zdeněk, I'm afraid that in this debate we have once again
reached an understanding of things that presumes the existence of certain exclusively socialist institutions connected only with socialist values. I propose that in connection with the questions that you have
raised we should proceed on the basis of a desire to synthesize various
historical periods, systems, and experiences. And not to forget that

only the free individual, not any institution, can be the true realization of socialist values.

Z.M.   I also consider that the natural starting point for our discussion. After all, perhaps the greatest defect of Leninism, and of Marxism in general, was that it perceived the working class as the subject of history, as an abstract category, and not as living people, individuals, and groups. Bolshevism crowned all of this with the conception that the main factor in achieving socialist goals was political power established in the name of this class. The theory of communism was definitely, in its essential features, utopian. But the responsibility of the Communist movement for the disasters and crimes of the totalitarian system begins only at that moment when it starts to operate on the basis of the conviction that its historical vision can be carried out only by means of a dictatorship involving political institutions, and by the suppression of all other conceptions and variations of social development.

But with the question I'm now asking I have something else in mind. What I am mainly interested in is this: What role do property relations and market relations have in the course of trying to achieve or implement socialist values? More than that, what institutions would facilitate and, contrariwise, what institutions would interfere with the goal that the majority of people, that is, all the people that depend upon earning a wage for their existence, would have maximum influence—both as individuals and as social groups—in deciding questions about the ends and means of developing the life of society in the present and the future?

M.G.   Many books have been written about property and the market, and I make no claim to any kind of new analysis. Let me just say briefly that when I think about this question I take into account all of the experience of Soviet planning, of perestroika, and the "shock therapy" implemented since 1991, and I try to evaluate the worldwide experience in this connection as far as I know it. The fundamental problem that I see is how to achieve a synthesis in this respect also among various conceptions and experiences, since one-sidedness has shown itself to be a chief cause of crisis and failure. The Achilles heel of socialism was the inability to link the socialist goal with the provision of incentives for efficient labor and the encouragement of initiative on the part of individuals. It became clear that in practice the market provides such incentives best of all. A market, of course, presupposes various property owners who are free to act as they wish, engage in competition, and so forth. By itself, however, the market places on the back burner a whole series of human needs, or fails to meet those needs altogether. And these human needs may be of the kind that from the point of view of socialist values are extremely important. Thus, these values unavoidably require a certain degree of regulation of the market. But how much regulation, what kind of regulation, by what means, to what extent, and in what areas of public life? Those questions can only be answered in accordance with the concrete situation. Invariably the answers will add up to a synthesis of various opinions and various interests. They will also depend on the material level, the general standard of living, political and cultural traditions, and other considerations that will vary from country to country. No one ideology, no one political party has the "only true recipe" in this regard.

Likewise, no one form of property in and of itself can overcome all problems. In practice we had only one form of property, state property, but it did not get rid of exploitation. And even though it was impossible to even install a toilet without permission from the planners, we did not succeed in efficiently planning our countries' economic development. In contrast, private multinational corporations, in which no one imposes decisions on the managers from the planning point of view, no one tells them what to do, have carried out quite efficient strategic planning in their spheres of activity. And of course in countries where public property or state-owned property is not at all dominant, nevertheless the governments do plan, and embody those plans in electoral platforms, and to some extent carry out those plans. And so in trying to solve such questions, it is necessary to proceed from the experiences of various systems and conceptions, to search for an optimal synthesis and not an ideological recipe offering universal salvation.

Z.M.   I agree, Misha. But I think this line of argument should be supplemented by a certain principle: whoever really wants to put socialist values into practice must effectively protect certain social needs—especially health care and education, and nowadays a whole range of environmental issues—from the effects of the so-called free market. To what extent and by what means will remain a specific problem in every situation, and it will require a synthesis of various approaches and interests.

Likewise, as far as forms of property are concerned, it would be correct to proceed from the inevitable pluralism of these various forms, but at the same time one principle needs to be observed: any form of property that acquires such a strong position that it is able to avoid democratic social control must nevertheless be subjected to such control. Otherwise its interests alone will be promoted without regard for the other needs of people in the society, and of course without regard for socialist values. This has to do with both private property and state property.

The problem of effective democratic forms of control has not been solved satisfactorily anywhere. But for the sake of socialist values it must be solved. I have become convinced of this by both the experience in the West and the post-1989 process of "building capitalism" in the Czech Republic and other countries. Also, of course, by the so-called shock therapy in Russia.

Democratic social control over the actions of the large owners of capital, whether private or public, is not a task for some special institution or a matter requiring extraordinary administrative measures. Properly speaking, it is the primary problem faced in the development of political democracy in modern-day society. There is of course no reason to have doubts about the basic principles of parliamentary pluralistic democracy—the separation of powers, government based on law, and other such basic building blocks of a democratic political system. The question is, isn't it worth trying to supplement the existing institutional forms of democracy with new ones? Are certain practical forms of parliamentarism sufficient? For example, the special position held by political parties as intermediaries between the citizen and the state. Are these sufficient to express new needs or to solve new problems? In the developed Western countries there are serious symptoms of a crisis of the political party structure in this sense and there have been for a long time.

I personally hold that a key role in all this is played by one's concept of the free individual. The individual for liberal ideologists is still essentially an abstraction. For them the free individual in the abstract is the subjective agent of history, just as the working class in the abstract was the primary agent of history for the Marxists. There is a similar one-sidedness in both views. After all, in historical reality the primary agent of history has been the individual who has been shaped to a significant extent by existing social relations. This applies both to every individual and to social groups in general.

For supporters of the socialist idea the main problem is this: What institutions in a democratic system will help to enhance the role of the socially determined individual, or more exactly, increase the influence of the majority who earn their living by wage labor? We don't have to go into organizational details, but on the practical plane it would be worth discussing this a little bit.

M.G.   These are questions, Zdeněk, which I also consider extremely important and I have been forced to seek answers to them more than once in the past. They were at the center of a recent discussion in Italy, because the tradition of leftist thought is strong there, but also a quite evident crisis of the political party structure has existed there for many years, and this is an urgent current problem. In that discussion I defended the viewpoint that today in advanced modern societies social structure has changed so much and the many diverse existing interests have become so complex that the oversimplified classical structure of political parties has become insufficient to express them. The oversimplified polarization of parties into right wing and left wing in the West has been inadequate for a long time, precisely because in the post-World War II period huge mass parties of the center began to develop—left center and right center parties. But this is a political structure that in many Western countries has now ceased to satisfactorily reflect the new situation.

And so to picture modern-day society in terms of the trivial sche-matic image of a conflict between two classes has actually not been possible for a long time now. It is necessary to search for a way of solving the problems of further development outside of this schematic framework. This also applies to the development of the institutions of a democratic society. Today I see a possibility for future development that holds great promise, and that is the concept of social partnership. Soviet ideology proclaimed this a betrayal of the working class, but in reality it can be one of the most effective ways of enhancing the real influence of wage labor in the making of political decisions. Also, a way of beginning to overcome the monopoly role of political parties in mediating relations between citizens and the state. To look for ways of developing the institution of social partnership where it has not yet been applied in my opinion is one of the specific answers to your ques-tion. Of course certain economic and social conditions would have to exist for this, and in many parts of the world they do not now exist. But in the countries of the former "actually existing socialism," in my opinion, the conditions do exist.

z.m.   I fully agree with you, but it is apparent that the neoliberal advocates of "building capitalism" and of the "pure market" would have quite a different opinion, whether they belong to the government circles of certain post-Communist countries or to the International Monetary Fund.

m.g.   Of course, and they would also be found in certain government circles in the West. I can tell you this, Zdeněk, while I was still president of the USSR and was meeting with heads of government of the G-7 countries [the Group of Seven, the seven wealthiest industrial coun-tries] I spoke quite openly about the fact that freedom of choice must naturally be extended to former Soviet society as well. That society, in my opinion, will continue to have a need for mixed forms of property relations, a mixed economy, and its own path of development as far as its political system goes. That is, it would not be possible to borrow or adopt the American or some other Western system. And I saw a shadow of doubt slip across the faces of George Bush and the Japanese at that point. Only the French president, Mitterrand, stated openly that as a socialist he supported my point of view.

z.m.   There is something else that can be connected with institutions of social partnership, and that is the role that can be played in a democratic system by so-called work collectives, or labor collectives (the work force at any given place of business conceived of as an assembly with democratic voice). These are communities of individuals that have been created by the division of labor, and their main interests tend to coincide, although sometimes in some places they conflict. Thus, for example, there is a highly significant contradiction between the interest that the work force has in receiving maximum pay and the interest it has at the same time in the achievement of an efficient and flourishing state of affairs at "its" factory, office, or other organization.

But it is precisely for these reasons that work collectives could have enormous significance in shaping the appropriate practices or habits necessary for solving problems through compromise and cooperation among various interest groups instead of intensification of conflict.

I think that the communities of people at various work places, not only factories but also health care institutions, educational institutions, and so forth, in modern society are an important agent of history. Unlike territorial communities, neighborhoods, or urban areas, the work forces at various places of employment are not usually perceived as the primary agents of the political system. In a certain sense it was precisely the Soviet type of society that created highly favorable conditions for work collectives to become such agents. Unfortunately a more or less significant attempt along these lines was made only in Yugoslavia, where for a number of special reasons the model of "workers' self-management" ultimately failed. It is interesting, however, that we find attempts to create institutions that would bring labor collectives into politics (various forms of factory councils, factory committees, workers' councils, and so forth) in every country where a democratic working class movement developed—for example, in

Czechoslovakia from 1945 to 1948 and then again in 1968; also in Hungary and Poland in 1956 and especially in Poland in 1980 and afterward. As you know, Misha, during the perestroika era I tried to influence you personally to give work collectives and bodies of workers' self-management an important role in the democratic political system in the USSR. But that was in 1990 and by then it was hardly possible to put the idea into practice. Today of course the conditions for doing that in the former countries of "actually existing socialism" are even less favorable than in other parts of the world, because the entire economic and social structure has been destroyed and is still in a state of flux. The ruling circles and a significant section of the rest of society have placed many other and very different problems first on the order of the day. In spite of that I still think that in modern society this is one of the possible paths of development for institutions that would help promote socialist values. What do you think about that today?

M.G.   This is a major question, full of contradictions, some of which you have already touched on. Moreover, this is a problem that not only socialists consider important. In the West, after all, there are a number of forms through which workers participate in decision making at various levels, from factory councils to advisory or supervisory bodies in major corporations. Strictly speaking, there are certain elements of self-management here, but at the same time they are linked with stock ownership, profit sharing, and so on. Efforts to encourage the work force to take an interest in the success of the given factory or institution are being made in all modern capitalist business establishments. In Japan this has taken rather unique forms, deriving from its own special traditions.

The extreme case of Yugoslavia warns us against overestimating the possibilities of self-management by the producers. The result in Yugoslavia was disintegration and destruction.

Z.M.   Yes, but Misha, in Yugoslavia the self-management model was immediately absorbed into a system in which a single political party held a monopoly of power and turned "self-management" into a means for maintaining its own domination. Moreover, the decentralization of self-management, although it did give great local powers to the national republics, nevertheless contributed to bureaucratic centralism within each of the republics of Yugoslavia. Because of this, nationalism took on greater importance, fed further by the inequality of living standards from one Yugoslav republic to another.

M.G.   I don't mean to oversimplify anything. I only want to emphasize that there is both positive and negative historical experience on this point. And in practice this problem makes itself evident both in economies that are primarily capitalist and in the various types of systems that have called themselves socialist. In our country too there were attempts to solve the problem, there was a law providing for work collectives, but unfortunately during the perestroika era they did not play a major role. I share the opinion that the solution to this problem is one of the most important aspects of creating new institutions, especially if they are to contribute to the implementation of socialist values.

Such institutions of workers' self-management do not by any means necessarily conflict with territorial self-management in urban areas and larger metropolitan regions. Developing workers' self-management and increasing the powers and the authority of local government I also consider the necessary line to follow in seeking to strengthen the democratic political system. This task has to do not only with socialist values, but nevertheless it is a primary concern of socialists. Therefore, properly speaking, the actual possibility for the largest possible number of citizens to actively involve themselves in political decision-making— that is also a socialist value. Not *only* socialist, of course, but it is a socialist value.

Z.M.   Yes, I agree, and I think that this is a specific area for possible cooperation between supporters of socialist and of liberal ideas. Because in most Soviet-type societies today the primary task is to form a structure of civil society. By this I mean, speaking in an oversimplified way, a structure of organizations, institutions, associations, and other kinds of groups that would operate in the space between the government and the individual. Institutions of self-management and self-government constitute a logical and necessary skeleton for civil society, a guarantee against bureaucratic centralism on the part of the government power. Between government interests and private interests there are social interests, and these, if they are not to be co-opted by government, can enter into politics precisely through, and only through, the structures of civil society. This is a conception that both liberalism and democratic socialism have in common.

M.G.   In this sense I am of course a proponent of the socialist idea, and not just of formal democracy. What is involved is a real possibility of choice for the people who actually live in a particular society, and who are part of its social structure in very specific ways.

Various Roads to Socialism in the Modern World

Z.M.   If we were to briefly summarize our present understanding of socialism we could say approximately the following: socialism is, first of all, a process of development, a particular tendency that seeks in industrial society (and in a future post-industrial society) to put into practice or implement values that are connected with the socialist idea.

M.G.   We both should publicly acknowledge the great mistake we made when as supporters of Communist ideology we denounced Eduard Bernstein's famous dictum: "The movement is everything, the ultimate goal nothing." We called that a betrayal of socialism. But the essence of Bernstein's idea was that socialism could not be understood as a system that arises as a result of the inevitable downfall of capitalism, but that socialism is a gradual realization of the principle of equality and self-determination for the people who constitute a society, an economy, a country.

Z.M.   Yes, Misha, we parroted many denunciations without knowing what we were condemning. If only this could serve as a lesson for those who are doing the same thing today, even if they are doing so in reverse and citing other "classical writings" as their justification. But let me go back to something that I didn't finish saying. It follows from our conception of socialism as a worldwide process that the values socialism wants to put into practice are everywhere similar and held in common. But apart from those values everything else can change according to circumstances, the circumstances in which processes and movements are developing, including the movements that advocate those values. And since the socialist tendency, like the capitalist tendency, cannot operate in just one or a few countries, but rather operates on a world scale, the completely different conditions from one country or one part of the world to another have a determining effect on what forms and in what places the socialist idea can influence the development of society. In our unified world, although there are not "two camps," there are on the other hand a number of different social, political, and cultural worlds concealed within that single unified world. Within each of them socialism is a worldwide process facing both general and specific tasks.

M.G.   I can illustrate this with a very specific example taken from my recent trip through Latin America. With my own eyes I saw conditions that are only capable of generating class struggle, such a frightening gap between rich and poor, such a division in society, with no possibility of social partnership at all. For many members of the public in those countries I was too right wing. You could hear shouts that I was a betrayer of socialism. What they want there is Fidel! But when I began to talk about the fact that government must perform social functions, eliminate mass poverty, and ensure equality and justice there was great applause and a favorable response. Another response was that the authorities took away the airplane that had been placed at my disposal earlier.

Z.M.   Today, given the effects of the impasse and downfall of the Soviet system, what is closest to us is the Western European form of the socialist movement, the welfare state created by Western Social Democracy, the institutions of social partnership, and everything else that we have been talking about. I think that in European countries this is justified. But when you look at this from the point of view of the world as a whole things are much more complicated. The Social Democratic parties have in their own way built a kind of "socialism in one country," that is, each has restricted itself to its own country. The result is incomparably more attractive than the Soviet model of socialism in one country, but for people in other countries it has had little or no meaning.

The Socialist International did not recognize the problem of the Third World as a major challenge for itself until the late 1970s, when the so-called Brandt commission [named after Willy Brandt, leader of the West German Social Democratic Party] began to consider that problem. Also certain new problems in the advanced Western countries have brought forces into political life that stand outside of the Social Democratic movement, for example, the Greens, the environmentalist movement that came into existence more to the left of Social Democracy. Nor can it be said today that there is any readymade Social Democratic recipe for solving the problems of former Soviet bloc countries. It seems to me that it's impossible for us, as people who overcame our own concept of a universal Communist recipe for historical development, to believe in the universal effectiveness of the ideas, methods, or experience of Western European Social Democracy.

M.G.   You're definitely right that socialism needs critical analysis, not only of the Soviet variant that led to totalitarianism, but of other variants, above all the Social Democratic one. Social Democracy itself ought, of course, to undertake such analysis. As everyone knows, any experience has both positive and negative sides. In my personal opinion positive elements prevail in the experience of Social Democracy. And although there can be no readymade recipe for the socialist perspective in the former lands of "actually existing socialism," on the other hand there are a great many fundamental lessons and incentives for further action.

z.m.   That's right, and a practical proof of that, besides, is the fact
that our own attempts to reform and revitalize socialism on fundamental questions were inspired precisely by the Social Democratic
road. But I had something else in mind. I would argue that Social
Democracy in the West was solving a historically distinct problem: in
a functioning capitalist system it became a factor of political pressure
through which the capitalist tendency was restricted and subjected to
regulation, so that it was forced to take into consideration, to a greater
extent, the interests of people who live by wage labor. The actual functioning of the economy, however, was still determined by capital.

In the West today, however, new problems confront society as a
whole, and it would seem they also confront the socialist movement.
And no one has provided satisfactory solutions to these problems.
From the point of view of socialist values, we are talking mainly about
three sets of problems.

First of all, there are several, by no means new, problems of social
inequality. The welfare state has ended up in a blind alley in a number
of areas because government spending connected with it has become
too large. The constantly increasing bureaucratization of the social
assistance apparatus has played a certain part in this. The proportion
of those dependent on social assistance has also grown. Unemployment
has not simply failed to decline; it has been increasing, with certain
categories of people in effect being left permanently unemployed. We
are not just talking about older people; young workers as well simply
cannot find jobs. As average longevity has increased, the number of
retirees receiving old-age benefits has grown quickly. The housing crisis
has also become a very important social problem. A situation has
arisen in the advanced industrial countries where a very numerous social group has taken shape, which Ralf Dahrendorf calls the "under-
class" and which, for all practical purposes, has no hope of improving
or changing its situation. The result of all this is that today in the
Western countries there is virtually a secret and sometimes open war
going on over maintaining the welfare state model. The question is:
Should the problem be solved by renouncing the social gains that have
been achieved? Or on the other hand, should the necessary expendi-

tures for maintaining the welfare state be covered by placing further restrictions on capital?

In the long-term perspective, even on the conceptual plane, the advanced Western countries face an unresolved problem: the social consequences of their very own success. It is a question of the future results that are already easily imaginable as the scientific and technological revolution continues to unfold in industry and other realms of social activity. Right now the so-called revolution in microelectronics is going on, as can be seen mainly in the computerization of practically every area of life. Also knocking on the door are practical problems resulting from the increased use of genetic engineering, and an expected revolution in the realm of energy and electric power. These processes at first give the impression of providing improved services for human beings, demonstrating the success of capitalism, but in reality they are harbingers of the forthcoming total destruction of the existing system of wage labor—the elimination, on a certain level, of human labor in general as a vital function of human society. The estimates of experts, although they vary, tend to agree that within twenty or thirty years the number of work sites that today employ physical labor or elementary mental labor, whether it be major mass production or administrative and service areas, will be reduced by 30–50 percent.

Inevitably this presupposes a fundamental change in the way social wealth is distributed. The decisive criteria for the distribution of wealth in the distant future will no longer be able to rest on questions of property or ownership, nor on wages for labor, because distribution on that basis would simply be insufficient for everyone. To solve this problem it will not be enough for humankind in the future to make use of the model of present-day Western civilization, nor the ideological conceptions of either the traditional right or the traditional left, whether radical and revolutionary or reformist.

It will also not be possible to solve ecological problems satisfactorily within the framework of the existing model of the welfare state even if it were to overcome its present crisis.

The socialist tendency—precisely because it will express general human interests and not just narrow group interests—will also be forced to solve such problems, even though today they seem unsolvable. In this way I wish to emphasize that the conception of socialism as "global humanism" of the future cannot rest upon the present perception of the ideas and practices of Social Democracy. Although these have been successful in the past, today they are in many respects powerless in the face of the fundamental contradictions that the future holds for the more advanced countries.

M.G.   But all of this, Zdeněk, is directly connected to the overall civilizational development of the present-day world. And so we will return to this question also when we take up the question of global interconnectedness. The Gorbachev Foundation from the very beginning of its activity set as one of its main tasks the goal of working out the problems of a transition to a new paradigm of development—or, as we call it, a new civilization. We have reported on our first strictly preliminary conclusions at various international conferences. But if we are to speak only about the main conclusion we came to as early as the very beginning of our research, this is that such a transition is possible only on the basis of a reassertion of general human values, of course as they are interpreted and applied in the present historical context, and taking into account global challenges that the world community cannot avoid responding to. And that is the key for each individual nation in deciding its national goals in this crucial stage of human history.

3. AT A CROSSROADS OF CIVILIZATION

Neither Yalta, nor Malta

Z.M.   Many people both in the West and the East, on the left and on the right, are under the impression now that with the end of the Cold War what dominates the world above all is a great uncertainty. Developments have become less predictable; political events and their consequences less subject to calculation. Things have passed beyond the control of the superpowers that at one time more or less kept them under control, because one of those superpowers, the USSR, has ceased to exist. It might seem that this would result in a situation in which the United States, as the only existing superpower, would end up in a simpler position because supposedly it could control world developments without confronting a rival. In reality, however, the United States has no effective means of asserting such control, especially in the former sphere of influence of the USSR. The result has been a visible loss of certainty and increased unpredictable risks. I think, Misha, that although to a certain extent the loss of the "certainty" that existed in the era of stagnation was a necessary price that had to be paid to have a free forward movement, the present state of affairs is something that neither side in the Cold War originally desired.

M.G.   This is by no means a new problem. I have already spoken publicly on this subject several times. You yourself, Zdeněk, took part in the Gorbachev Foundation conference on prospects for a greater Europe held in December 1992. I cannot, of course, repeat everything that was said there. Europe and in fact the whole world for many years during the Cold War became used to the situation, to a condition that I call confrontational stability. In those days it was clear who stood on which side of the barricades. Both groups were armed to the teeth, and there was a special kind of closing of the ranks in the event of any perceived danger arising from the other side. A great many problems of internal development within each of the opposing blocs, as well as contradictions on the regional and international scale, were pushed into the background because of this situation. The confrontation between two opposing blocs thus gave rise to discipline within each bloc, and thus on both sides "order" was strengthened. Within the totalitarian regimes this served as the basis for suppressing any kind of "deviation" whatsoever; any critical disagreement with the policies of the ruling circles was seen as, or portrayed as, betrayal and as "deserting to the other side."

Yes, we succeeded in not allowing a war to happen. However, that situation not only resulted inevitably in stagnation and a militarized economy (not only in the USSR, by the way), but in many other undesirable consequences that were impossible to maintain except with the use of force. The international relations that existed then created only the appearance of certainty, because the only certainty was the fact that the "governability" of the world was based on the force of arms, on the ability to destroy life on earth, and on fear of such a catastrophic outcome. To save humanity from this fear and the possibility of such a disaster, and at the same time to preserve a sense of security or certainty that was based on such fear, was simply impossible.

z.m.   I agree. That is exactly what I had in mind when I spoke about the present risks as the price paid for freeing ourselves from the dead end of the Cold War. This is the old and well-known contradiction between the security of a prison and the risk of freedom. Nevertheless, I suppose that when you and George Bush met on the island of Malta at the end of 1989 and took a definitive political step toward ending the Cold War, you imagined future developments differently. You have published excerpts from the talks you had at that time, and it is possible, in a one-sided way, to demonstrate from those excerpts that your jointly held conceptions coincided, among other things, on the idea that from then on the world would be more easily and rationally governable. The idea also seemed to be that the United States and the USSR wanted to cooperate because it was more rational to "govern" the world jointly, in accordance with the specific rules and needs of this unified world, however contradictory it might be—and on the basis of generally recognized democratic values.

m.g.   If the published materials about the Malta talks are to be mentioned, Zdeněk, I want to immediately warn against any attempt to interpret the Soviet initiative at those talks as any kind of project for creating a Soviet-American condominium, or joint Soviet-American rule over the world.

z.m.   I had absolutely no intention of using the word "govern" in that pejorative sense. I have no doubt whatsoever that Malta was an attempt to overcome Yalta, that is, the concept of the division of the world into exclusive spheres of influence, into "two camps." After all, the starting point was the idea that the USSR and the USA would remain the two decisive forces in resolving global problems. However, as time went by, with the disintegration of the USSR and of the Soviet bloc, a state of affairs emerged that was neither Yalta nor Malta.

M.G.   Fine, I accept your explanation, but I want to continue the discussion about Malta because it is not without interest. Of course we could not foresee all the consequences of the ending of the Cold War; such things are beyond anyone's capacity. The important thing is that even then we foresaw that the transition to a new state of affairs in the world would be difficult and full of risks, in particular in the countries of Eastern Europe. It was my view, moreover, that interference in these complex processes from the standpoint of someone's one-sided interests was simply impermissible and would be fraught with great complications. Such profound changes required a philosophical-political approach, and an understanding of the historical scale on which these things were happening. So I was very far from any idea that after Malta, Bush and I would be able to "regulate history" through telephone conversations.

Z.M.   All right, but although you didn't think in that way, that doesn't mean that many other people weren't reasoning along those lines. There's something else of interest to me. In my opinion, back then, in December 1989, it was entirely justifiable to think that the USA and the USSR were in quite an exceptional position, with great possibilities and responsibility for all of world politics. It was therefore natural that the presidents of those two countries should seek to come to agreement in principle on ways of cooperating and solving the problems of world politics. I merely think that agreements of this kind had a realistic and binding political character because each side perceived the other as an equal power, and neither side could allow itself to underestimate the other. That is what in fact made agreements binding on both. Unfortunately, the USSR was only an equal partner of the USA in one respect—military force. And because, by their very nature, such agreements reduced the importance of military power in world politics, since that was a precondition for ending the Cold War, Soviet steps in that direction unavoidably resulted in the ultimate weakening of its own position in relation to the United States. In other words, the USSR could not achieve its own goals without sawing off the proverbial branch it was sitting on during its negotiations with the United States. But no one at Malta presumed any such outcome and neither of the participants desired it.

M.G.   I think your line of argument is open to criticism. The potential of the USSR as a whole would have allowed it to be a genuine partner of the United States, and successful reforms would only have contributed to that.

At the same time, Zdeněk, in order to understand the complicated nature of developments since Malta it must be kept in mind that the modern world is at a turning point, seeking the road toward a new civilization.

We Are Living at a Time of Crisis of Civilization

Z.M.   We are thus approaching once again a number of questions that we have recently discussed, although of course from a different angle. The main question is whether it will be possible after the end of the Cold War between East and West to resolve, without confrontations or wars, other serious conflicts arising out of our existing civilization. In the first place there are the flagrant inequalities between the wealthy countries and the poor countries, between the North and the South, between less than 20 percent of the human race and more than 80 percent. These inequalities, contradictions, and potential conflicts are not only economic, social, and political but also ecological and of a cultural-civilizational character. I am not a proponent of catastrophic scenarios or apocalyptic ideas, but I think that it will be impossible to find a satisfactory solution on the basis of the contemporary version of Western civilization. But that is only one of many aspects of the problem.

M.G. I had the opportunity of meeting with [former U.S. Secretary of State] George Shultz in the United States in 1992, by which time neither of us any longer held a government post. He is a man of great experience and abilities, capable of accepting the views of others and considering them and acknowledging what is rational in them; he is simply not blinded by ideological preconceptions. We met, along with some close collaborators, for a frank discussion. When our debates touched on demographic problems the question arose whether in general the further development of the world on the basis of contemporary tendencies of Western civilization is possible. I reminded the participants in the discussion that at one time we had come to the conclusion that it was impermissible to try to impose the Soviet model and we adhered to that conclusion in the policies of perestroika. Under different historical circumstances the Soviet system had been imposed by force, and we rejected the possibility of trying to maintain it by force. I then expressed the idea that the Americans should follow this example and acknowledge the principle of freedom of choice for all people and for all nations. At this point I said that the American way of life was of course a unique phenomenon, but it had been achieved at a price that could be paid only by way of exception. I reminded my listeners that today the United States uses approximately 44 percent of the energy in the world, and only a little more than half remains for the rest, who number approximately 5 billion people. It is not just a question of economic potential. The great progress and prosperity in the United States is accompanied by moral degradation, the growth of drug addiction, crime, and antisocial tendencies. That is why Western civilization, whose summit is precisely the American way of life, provides no satisfactory answer to the question: Which road of development should world civilization take?

Z.M. You know, Misha, here's an interesting thing. The view you've just expressed is entirely consistent with what Zbigniew Brzezinski said in his book *Out of Control,* published in 1993. This is a man who absolutely cannot be suspected of leanings toward communism or socialism or anti-American views or naiveté. He is in fact a realist whose outlook borders on cynicism. His overall conception is of course different from yours or mine. It proceeds from the idea that the United States will, for the foreseeable future, remain the only global power. He thinks that it is unrealistic, however, for America to try to fulfill this "historic mission" if it cannot deal with its own crisis of civilization. He describes the crisis of the American way of life in twenty specific points, approximately half of which have to do with economic inadequacies, social policy, and party politics, while the other half have to do with values, morality, and the meaning of life.

The main source and common denominator in the degeneration of civilization, as Brzezinski sees it, is in effect that the chief motive for human behavior has become immediate satisfaction of material needs and individual desires, that a tolerant attitude toward insatiable greed has produced this kind of "actually existing" morality; thus, a society has grown up in which one can have everything, and for the sake of achieving that, everything is permitted. The growing and all-encompassing sense of moral emptiness, in his opinion, prevents present-day America from being able to play a decisive and constructive role in global civilizational changes.

M.G.   All this merely confirms what we have already said: if the solution was merely that the whole world should live the way people now live in the West, the human race could not avoid new conflicts and new attempts to resolve contradictions or conflicts of interest by military force, to defend the privileges of the wealthy through the use of force, or else to use force and violence to bring about a redistribution of wealth in favor of the poor. An arms race would start up again and ultimately war would threaten once again, including nuclear war, which would mean the destruction of life on earth. But that would not be a solution to the crisis of civilization; it would be a catastrophe. The only real way out would be a new era of civilization, the beginning of an entirely new epoch, but that would require finding a new common paradigm, a new conception of the foundations of civilization, one capable of avoiding the deformations and degeneration that the present Western model is leading us to. It is a question of a civilization that would not end in self-destruction in either societal or ecological respects. But the condition for this, in my opinion, is a change of values. Until we change our value orientation we will change nothing.

Z.M.   I agree with that. Only I foresee so many obstacles on the road to this that I regard the prospects for the near future with great skepticism. If there are people who generally perceive the seriousness of the crisis of the Western way of life, as well as the lack of realism in its simply being adopted by the rest of the world, still this only constitutes a minority in the societies that have come to know this lifestyle in practice. For billions of others this remains a desirable vision; people simply want to live in a similar way. And they can come to understand only through their own experience that this is a chimerical vision. But that won't happen precisely because the goal itself is unrealistic. And since this is so, the West should not try to impose its lifestyle as the only one worth imitating. Instead, the West ought to take purposeful action to counter the illusion that its "model" is realistic for the rest of the world. But it is hard to imagine this happening. Because, aside from anything else, what is involved here above all are not moral problems and not even ideological problems in general, but the material interests of capital and the world market.

M.G.   Yes, of course there is a great danger here that we will begin to lag behind intellectually and politically in relation to the problems involved in the development of a new civilization. I see a certain analogy with the course that perestroika took in our country. If we limit ourselves merely to correct statements and don't carry out political and institutional changes in a timely fashion, changes that would be indispensable for implementing our conceptions, we could miss out on a historical opportunity.

Z.M.   What do you mean by "we" in this context?

M.G.   By this I mean for now the Europeans, all of Europe. After all, it's because we reached common ground with the Paris Declaration of

1990, but failed to create any effective institution to ensure adherence to its principles, that we missed the chance to prevent the tragedy in Yugoslavia. If in the future there is still no understanding of the need for fundamental change in the content and methods of politics, if groundbreaking changes don't affect the main political centers (Europe, the G-7 countries, the United Nations) there is a threat that we will not succeed in avoiding a new conflict. Fortunately, the extensive contacts I have show that many people belonging to truly influential circles in the West are aware of the crisis of the present-day Western way of life.

z.m.   Although I do not underestimate this, I have a skeptical comment. The ruling political circles in the West today, as we have already noted, too often have a sense of themselves as the victors in the Cold War. And the winning side in a war can allow itself to dismiss criticism, to refuse any change in what, to that side, seems to be what won the war and what thereby demonstrated its correctness. To exaggerate somewhat, when the victorious Soviet system after World War II began to believe that the victory had definitively proven the "superiority of socialism over capitalism," that viewpoint remained operative for quite awhile. My fear is simply that the politics of the powerful in this world will not make any fundamental innovations on a timely basis without a great deal of pressure.

m.g.   Any chance, of course, can be missed. But that does not mean that, in general, we should fail to take note of an opportunity and try to make use of it. I know that in our conversations you have leaned more toward skepticism and pessimism than optimism. But here is an example of a recent experience I had, an opportunity to have a debate within a small group of influential people in France.

And it was precisely from among them that I heard the argument that the West had already reached the upper limit of its possibilities and had nothing more to offer. One person said that now the answer must come from the "Russian cauldron." Although Russia today is in an extraordinarily complicated situation, Europe and the whole world need its answers to the new challenges. Russia has the necessary potential, both material and spiritual, for that. It does not have to imitate the West; it can propose new orientations, which it can see precisely because of what it has gone through as a country and is going through today.

Let me just add something to that for my own part: today the exact opposite is actually happening in Russia. Following the precepts of the International Monetary Fund, efforts are being made to adjust everything to the IMF's demands, to duplicate Western models, and to throw out our entire complex and valuable experience, the Soviet experiment, and to denounce it all as harmful ballast. This is a mistake on both the philosophical and the political level, which leads to a conflict with society, because it is in conflict with our people's mentality, culture, and needs. The liberal ideologists display a nihilistic attitude toward the past, whereas in fact the past should be utilized, including that part of it that is linked with socialist values.

z.m. In my opinion, Misha, this is precisely what could become a valuable contribution from the "Russian cauldron." Russia does belong to the mainstream of European civilization, but within its own limits it has exceptional features. First of all, while Russia is Europe, it is not only Europe. [A huge part of Russia is of course in Asia.] Besides that, it is the only part of Europe (along with some of the former Warsaw Pact countries) that can avail itself of the unique experience of having carried out a historical experiment—the revolutionary replacement of capitalism with socialism and communism. The very idea of such an experiment is part of European civilization and its cultural tradition, even though in Russia this turned out to be a totalitarian dictatorship costing millions of lives and ending in an impasse historically.

Elements of socialist values in the European sense did play a role in this, and a noncapitalist society of a special kind did arise. All this unrepeatable and valuable material in the "Russian cauldron" is still relevant today, in my opinion, in a process that involves all of Europe, as well as all the world, in the search for new paths for the development of civilization.

The main problem—and the main source of my skepticism—is in the realm of social practice, economic and political. A new type of civilization would necessarily require a fundamental change in the customary role of capital, and in the role of political power (including military power), as well as in the existing instruments and methods for "ruling the world." These are the three main neuralgic points, or most painful areas, in the present-day practices of our civilization, points at which its tendency toward self-destruction are most clearly displayed. Capital, left to its own devices, and without any effective control by society on a world scale, is the chief source of the destructive polarization between North and South in our world. And it plays a decisive role (directly and indirectly) in the growing threat to the global environment. Political power also has the destructive tendency to become self-contained and self-serving, turning into an instrument for the imposition of total control over the lives of individuals and the use of force for solving conflicts, up to and including the threat of nuclear war. Under such conditions the desire for "world government" remains above all a desire to take control of the world on behalf of certain centers where capital and power are concentrated. A new type of civilization would have to take measures in these three highly painful areas in order to gradually rule out such self-destruction by our civilization.

Can the World Be Governed Rationally?

M.G.   I think, Zdeněk, that on the basis of our very own striving over many years to make reforms within the framework of the Communist movement we have the right—and perhaps also the obligation—to say something about how we see the main errors and reasons for the collapse of Communist efforts to "rule the world and govern history." I place this entire phrase in quotation marks because in fact we are not talking about some single center "ruling" the world by issuing orders.

But it was, in fact, ultimately such a conception that Communist policy degenerated into in practice. This was the international aspect of Stalinism and the Soviet system of governing society by administrative command. The fundamental error was the idea that a certain ideology, certain values, and certain class interests are the exclusive vehicles for, or provide the only correct means of, deciding world problems. Historical experience has shown precisely the opposite: only by the cooperation of various kinds of decisions, different approaches to problems, can the world's knotty problems be unraveled in practice. Also in practice this is a process of gradual change, not a one-time revolutionary transformation. There is no magic ironing device that can "smooth out" all unpleasant conflicts and disparities in the world.

z.m.   And there is no supreme objective law of history that can provide a particular outcome for the human race. That will depend on humanity's mode of operation in relation to nature, and how people act toward one another.

m.g.   One should never base oneself on the idea that everything has been predetermined for human beings. Not only the existentialists but even Dostoevksy was right concerning schematic Communist ideas resulting in policies that overlooked the fact that humans are creative beings, that every individual creates his own world. People can make their own history if they have the material conditions for that and if they are guided by value orientations that do not lead to the destruction of society. This is the source from which I personally draw my optimism, because if something is possible it makes sense to strive toward it.

z.m.   Well, Misha, I must admit that that's exactly the reason why I sometimes give in to skepticism and pessimism. The desire to "rule the world" from positions of strength is, after all, not something that the Bolsheviks and Stalin invented on the basis of their deterministic doctrine. The entire history of European civilization consists of a series of such attempts: the Roman Empire in ancient times, the Crusades in the

Middle Ages, and colonialism in the modern era. And this was always based on the conviction that European civilization in its then-current form was the highest in comparison to the rest of the world, and therefore it had the right to dominate the world. Our civilization has never displayed a desire to seek some sort of synthesis or "third way" acceptable to all the world unless it was forced to do so by history. In this sense even the downfall of the seemingly all-powerful totalitarian government of the Soviet type is, strictly speaking, an exceptional case, because this gigantic political and military force left the stage of history in a generally peaceful way.

M.G.   Aside from anything else, that is exactly why I am an optimist today. A sense of the interconnectedness and unity of the whole world has caught hold with everyone; everyone is forced to recognize that no matter what happens anywhere in the world, we ourselves are affected. I think this provides the basic prerequisites for forward movement in the direction of new kinds of social relations and a new stage of civilization. But there are many different variations that such a movement could take.

Z.M.   Yes, and among them are pessimistic variations.

M.G.   Most likely. I do not, after all, rule out the possibility of catastrophe. Still, it was an understanding of the possible disaster of nuclear war that served as an incentive for me to arrive at the new thinking of perestroika. Let me ask you a simple question, Zdeněk: Should we just sit still, with arms folded, because of the danger of failure and catastrophe?

Z.M.   I'm not saying that at all, Misha, and in my life, I've never been guided by such thinking, no more than you have. Otherwise both of us might have remained sitting in some comfortable armchair, you in Moscow and I in Prague. Skepticism is necessary nevertheless in one's thinking; it leads not to passivity but to an awareness of risks; it acts as a corrective against any overestimation of one's powers. But let us

return to the specific question: In present-day reality what do you see
as an effective possibility for limiting world capital when it is acting
plainly against the needs of a new type of global civilization?

M.G.   First of all, Zdeněk, I would like clarification on what we mean
by limiting capital, or placing restrictions on it. Solidarity by the
wealthier countries with the poorer ones should not be taken to mean
a redistribution of wealth resulting in equality of poverty, as in the old
Communist conception. The wealthier and more developed countries
should understand that solidarity serves their own interests, that over
the long term they themselves cannot keep living as they would like
unless the standard of living of others is raised. We had a discussion
about this once with President Mitterrand of France. I asked him as a
socialist and as a friend to answer one question frankly: Why have
some individual capitalists understood long ago that they cannot simply strive to maximize the profits of the moment? In order to have
profits not just today but tomorrow as well, they ought to pay as high
a wage as possible and on the whole contribute to a rising level of
education and prosperity for the people, who after all ought to be their
best paying customers, and so on. Some individual capitalists have
already understood this, although of course that was under pressure
from socialists. But why in the world aren't capitalists as a whole able
to understand this? After all, by what it is doing in regard to the Third
World, world capital is sawing off the very branch it's sitting on.

Mitterrand answered me on this point: "I agree with you, but don't
try to apply that to France!" But he said that just to lighten the atmosphere. In general this is of course one of the most serious problems
we face, but I think it's possible to find instances that attest to the
possibility of solving this problem as well: gradually, in various ways
under varying circumstances, moving forward patiently along the road
of reform. Reforms also, after all, constitute a form of pressure, but
they require considerable time to succeed.

Z.M.   But that's exactly what I'm afraid of, that Western civilization
doesn't have an abundance of time left.

M.G.   Possibly time is short, but we cannot change that. Nevertheless I see certain real processes under way that offer hope. First of all, there is the entire development of capitalism since the nineteenth century, and especially since World War II. We have already noted that capitalism is not the same as it was originally, that a different kind of social structure exists and a different form of property, and of government regulation. The liberals have shown greater ability to react to new challenges than we socialists and communists have. We were too much imprisoned by our doctrine, wearing ideological blinders. They, on the other hand, displayed considerable initiative and an ability to make use of certain socialist values and instruments, so that under the pressure of practical need they began to allow the possibility of government regulation and intervention in the operations of capital. In other words, the possibility of cooperation, synthesis, and compromise between various approaches was demonstrated in practice, and proved useful for everyone. If that was possible on the level of the advanced capitalist countries, which serve as a "microcosm" relative to the rest of the world, why should that possibility be excluded on the "macro-level," on the world scale? Lastly, they have shown the capacity for creating effective regulating structures on various international levels. The European Union today is the result of a long process, which began with mutually advantageous economic integration, and its ultimate aim is the creation of a "greater Europe," which would be one of the main agents for the development of a new civilization in the modern world.

At least there is such a possibility and a real trend in that direction. It's true that this possibility could be missed, but it also could be realized. That is only one example; a number of international institutions have arisen that have the capability of influencing the functioning of world capital.

Z.M.   That may be so, but it is obvious from the example of the International Monetary Fund and its role in the Third World and in the "post-Communist countries" that Western capital is playing the leading role for all practical purposes.

M.G.   Of course that is true, but we are talking about the need to change the decisive direction and goals of international economic and political institutions to serve the global needs of the present world, which people are only beginning to become aware of. It is true that such a process is only in its beginning stages and no one can guarantee that it will be successful, but for me it is important that this process is today much farther along than it was twenty years ago. And this must be supported in every possible way. I see two dangerous extremes: on the one hand, a desire to issue orders and commands to the entire world from one center of power; and on the other, the hope that, all by itself, without human effort, the world will find the optimal path forward. I do not think that chaos in society is the way to reach the birth of a new order—and here, incidentally, I hold the same point of view that Lenin did. If the world were to develop solely along chaotic, or "spontaneous," lines, a pessimistic outcome could not be avoided.

Although in practice the results of efforts toward international coordination have often been really inadequate concerning very important questions, nevertheless the processes of integration and cooperation are going forward. Not always on a world scale but, let us say, within major regions. After all, economic integration in Western Europe started with agreements on coal and steel production, and has now reached the point where the European Union has become an integrated group of countries, so that Western Europe is now one of the major economic and political forces in the world. The motive force behind this, of course, was that the participants were seeking their own advantage, and not the smallest consideration in all this were the circumstances of the Cold War, but the results far exceed the intention of those original motivations. As long as Europe has the ability on this basis to achieve agreements integrating its eastern part into this process, it will have the prospect of playing a significant role in resolving global problems. But of course it may also miss this opportunity and thereby encourage the East Europeans to make their own attempts at integration.

On the worldwide level I would not underestimate the possibilities of the United Nations. However, some notable change in the direction of its activities would be required. Today it pays more attention to arguments over minor or partial issues than it does to global problems; it engages in endless speech making instead of trying to have an effect on world problems.

Z.M.   But even if the USSR still existed, Misha, and even if you as the president of the USSR managed to have questions placed on the UN agenda, an open question would still remain: Who would finance such projects?

M.G.   That too is one of the questions that the United Nations must resolve. I of course cannot answer that question now, but that does not mean that the UN would not be able to play a substantially more significant role in solving world problems on the conceptual level. Not always as an administrative institution but above all as a politically authoritative forum for discussion, for the consideration of different variants and arriving at a worldwide consensus.

In addition to everything that I have said, there are also possibilities for international cooperation in solving very specific problems that would be selected in a purposeful way. As president of the organization Green Cross International I have called for an environmental code to be worked out along with a set of new standards for international law that would govern environmental problems. I know that you could immediately start asking me ironical questions: Would countries abide by these regulations, let's say, the United States? Or would it be guided by the documents of the Rio de Janeiro conference on environmental problems? I see another aspect of the matter: the United States placed itself in an isolated position at the Rio conference, and for a number of reasons it does not feel comfortable with that. This will motivate the United States, over the course of time, to change its position. Of course we do not know when that will occur.

Z.M.   Again we are confronted with the time factor. If change depended on the effectiveness of measures taken by international organizations, if world development were to take place on an analogy with the post-World War II period of "social peace" in the Western countries, which I personally consider impossible because the conditions are not at all comparable, but if that were to be so, then in the best of cases billions of people in the Third World would have to wait for another half century. Do you think that that's acceptable for them and that they will be agreeable to that?

M.G.   We are starting to look at things now, Zdeněk, in somewhat the same way that used to be done decades ago in the USSR. As though there were a single entity called the Third World that constitutes a potential threat. We even viewed China back then as a potential enemy numbering one billion people who might have to be stopped by force of arms. We cannot close our eyes to practical experience. South Korea was quite a different country at one time than it is today: it was backward economically and politically, where now it is in the front ranks among economically prosperous countries, and politically it is on the road to democratization. The same with Thailand and Malaysia. We cannot simply expect that all the countries of Asia will suddenly have a rise in their standard of living as a single unit. Individual countries will gradually emerge from poverty. After all, China today is capable of feeding its people who number more than one billion . . .

Z.M.   But in China there is still a system of the Soviet type or close to it. So we should talk about it as a special case.

M.G.   All right, let's go to the American continent. I have already mentioned my impressions from a trip through Latin America, and why it is understandable that their expectations are connected with the hope for a political leader of the Castro type. But here again situations differ from country to country. Mexico already has the worst behind it. Chile is also on the verge of a major change, and I think that Argentina will also make a breakthrough, rising out of poverty. The situation in Brazil is not so simple. But I don't want to start making predictions or putting labels on individual countries. I will make one assertion: gradual development is possible in Latin America. How much time that will require is a judgment I do not dare to make. Of

course a development full of conflict is also possible, but that would
hardly open an appropriate road toward a new global civilization.

Besides, it seems to me that of decisive importance for development
in the so-called Third World is something else all together, something
we've already talked about, namely, the demographic factor. If there is
not success in fundamentally modifying the population explosion, and
if somewhere around the year 2020 the earth has ten billion people,
then I would think it likely that development ultimately would lead to
some sort of catastrophe, either economic, or environmental, or even
military. But the demographic factor changes as the result of change
on the levels of civilization and culture. It was easy to see this in the
former USSR: in the Baltic region, in Ukraine, and in Russia itself families with one or two children predominated, but from the Caucasus
region to Central Asia most families had five, eight, or ten children. So
unless the population explosion is regulated the new civilizational orientations and values, which the modern world needs so badly, are
hardly likely to appear. The world still has a chance to regulate itself
rationally but there is no guarantee other than living human beings,
and to lay the groundwork for people who can run the world rationally
requires changes in thinking and behavior. Politics by itself cannot
solve everything. Far from of it. Changes precisely on a civilizational
level are needed, a new way of life, values and standards to which
people's behavior will truly be subordinated in all parts of the world.

z.m.   I think that with the example of the population explosion you
have very accurately touched on the basic kind of problem that a new
global civilization will have to solve. It's a matter of self-limitation and
self-regulation by society in any or all forms of civilization. A matter
of self-limitation in relations among individuals in social groups,
classes, and nations and in their ideologies, for the sake of the common
global needs and interests of the human race. It's also a matter of self-
regulation by humankind as a whole in relation to nature in order to
preserve the necessary conditions for life on earth in the future. In
various parts of the world, and with various kinds of civilizations as a
basis, this self-limitation will differ in content. In some civilizations a

tradition is operative that says the more children there are, the greater the certainty for human survival. If people are to stop following that rule, they must have the experience of some other assurance of security in life.

All civilizational tendencies in the world need to change, but a change in Western civilization will have decisive importance, because its influence now dominates throughout the world. And its expansion has ultimately been the cause of one of the main global problems—the contradiction between the wealthy North and the impoverished South. This contradiction cannot be resolved peacefully unless today's wasteful Western society places a limit on its own demands, its pleasure-seeking egoism. The point is that, for economic, social, and environmental reasons, the billions of people on the earth simply cannot live like a privileged pack of egoists, even if they wanted to. Besides that, the end of the Cold War, which did away with the military form of the ideological conflict between "two camps," did not remove military force from the stage of history.

It operates as before in other kinds of conflicts, often traditional ones; and a serious risk for many regions of the world and for all of humanity remains linked with the use of military force. It is necessary that this be dealt with in the very first stage of the road toward a new global civilization. In the preliminary phase of this first stage many "new-old" conflicts will appear, in particular, national, racial, ethnic, and religious conflicts. It is worth noting, however, that in practice only here or there do such conflicts lead to a desire for an old-fashioned solution, with the use of force and violence and the resort to war (for example, in some areas of the former USSR and Yugoslavia). At the same time in other places, strange as it may seem, hopes for the possibility of new methods of solving conflicts are growing stronger (for example, in South Africa and some steps that have been taken in the Arab-Israeli conflict). Let me refer once again to the book by Brzezinski, because one of the concluding arguments in that book coincides with your view and mine: the desire to gain control over the collective fate of humanity will achieve success or failure mainly on the philosophical-cultural plane. In this regard Brzezinski assigns decisive importance to social self-regulation.

This self-regulation arises when people inwardly accept restrained views on what is appropriate and what is not, what is permissible and what is not.

It goes without saying that the capacity for such self-control or self-limitation will grow and develop, even in the best of cases, in a very uneven way in different parts of the world. And as we have already noted, different levels of priority will be assigned to this process. In some places regulation of the tendency of capital to maximize profit will prove to be of foremost concern; in other places birth control will come first; in still other places, for example, where Islamic fundamentalism is strong, the foremost concern will be to overcome religious fanaticism and replace it with tolerance.

The development of a global civilization in practice will proceed in a framework in which several different centers of different civilizations will exist, and they in turn will each consist of several different political groups or blocs of countries.

It's absolutely indisputable from this point of view that there will be an American group dominated by the United States and embracing virtually the entire Western Hemisphere. Further, there will be a European group, the eastern part of which will only assume its final shape in connection with the development of Russia (and correspondingly, the development of the other former Soviet republics). In Asia roughly two groupings can be delineated: an East Asian grouping (China and Japan, with influence on the Pacific region all the way to Australia); and a South Asian one (dominated by India). Also included in Asia would be an Islamic grouping, which would look like an odd aggregation of countries having few resources economically or politically but stretching from North Africa across the Persian Gulf to Central Asia. Within each of these groupings, for all practical purposes, there are fairly well-developed countries from the point of view of modern capitalism as well as so-called developing countries. Thus, not only the Third World, but also the First World cannot be conceived of as a single whole or a single unit in either the territorial or the civilizational sense.

From the point of view of the unifying theme of our conversations, that is, from the point of view of our conception of socialism, I would like to conclude with a few more comments. Socialism, too, as a world-wide process, lives and operates in practice within the framework of this division of the world into various centers of civilization and political groupings. In the United States, as we have already noted, it does not exist in the form of a politically significant independent movement, and its value orientations are partly expressed within the framework of the liberal democratic ideological conception. In Europe today, after the collapse of the Communist movement, socialism survives above all in the form of the Western European Social Democratic movement. In the former countries of "actually existing socialism" for the most part socialism still has an insufficiently politically formed aspect, but on the whole, things are moving toward some sort of variation on the Western European type. In Latin America socialism operates as a mixture of radical-revolutionary and reformist movements, with the constantly weakening influence of a variation on the Soviet model exerted through Cuba.

Socialism as a worldwide process is in a different situation in Asia, considering the fact above all of the existence of a certain variant of the Soviet system in China. (North Korea and Vietnam have no independent importance.) After the death of Mao Zedong China has oriented toward modernization in the sense of adopting the Western dynamic, particularly through the mediation of Japan. Speaking in terms of the former "Communist world," we can say that China has practically become, since approximately 1978, a pioneer of that very revisionism which was so strongly condemned by Maoism. However, in 1989 military and police violence was used to suppress an attempt by radical groups, particularly students, to step across a boundary in the process of modernization beyond which the Communist Party would have relinquished its monopoly on power. Chinese society today, like the former Soviet society, combines within itself certain elements and social relations that are both socialist and nonsocialist, including precapitalist, as well as those of a capitalist nature. It is hard to say what the proportions and relative weight of these various elements are, but I think it is indisputable that the significance of the socialist elements here is greater than in other Asian countries.

Thus, China introduces into a civilizational milieu beyond the bounds of Western civilization certain value orientations that are in fact of European origin. There is a contradiction between the acceptance of these socialist elements and the rejection of others, for example, the European conception of the inalienable natural rights of every individual—and this contradiction is glaringly evident. However, many other countries in the non-Western spheres of civilization share with China this rejection of the Western concept of human rights, so that this cannot simply be equated with arbitrary dictatorial rule of the Stalin type. Such an element most likely does exist, but what is primarily involved is a contradiction between civilizational traditions and the current developmental needs of both China and the present-day West. The results are contradictory: on a basic Third World question, birth control, China has achieved undoubted success. This of course serves the interests of the West and of future global civilization, although the methods by which this success has been achieved often do not conform to the criteria of humanism.

Therefore I have no answer to the question whether the present social and political system in China will end up the same way as the USSR. It may, to the contrary, become one of the most important tendencies in the process of creating a new civilization, and not only in China.

M.G.   You weren't wishing, were you, that once again we would have the answer to every question?

The Conscience of the Reformer

z.m   At the conclusion of our conversations, Misha, it would probably be worth saying a few words about how we ourselves, on a completely subjective level, experienced the rather high drama represented
by the attempt to reform "actually existing socialism."

There were several months of the Prague Spring, in which I had a
personal role, and there were six years of perestroika, in which you
had a personal role—although of course these two things cannot be
equated in terms of historical and political importance. But as far as
our subjective experiences, our purely personal impressions and sen-
sations, are concerned, it may very well be that the differences in scale
aren't decisive and that there is a great deal in common. Here too I
would try to formulate some of my experiences and feelings after 1968
and to tell about a certain inner voice of conscience that confronted
me with quite a few questions. And I would like to hear whether you
perceive things in a similar fashion or, on the contrary, view them differently.

m.g.   I would agree with that, Zdeněk. It's worth talking about.

Would We Do It Again?

z.m   After 1968 I was tormented for a long time by the knowledge
that, regardless of my intentions, after the suppression of the Prague
Spring the situation, not just for Czechs and Slovaks, but for all democratic socialist politics in general, became much worse than it had
been previously. And there's no getting around it: even though military
intervention was the result of someone else's decision, not mine—even

though Brezhnev bore the responsibility, not I—nevertheless, intervention happened precisely because I, along with others, tried to carry
through policies that Moscow reacted against in just that way.

The question of assigning blame in such cases is not the only question because, as is well known, you can be "at fault" without being
entirely "to blame." For that reason for several years I kept asking
myself over and over again: Wouldn't it have been better, strictly speaking, not to have undertaken any such experiments at all? Just to have
waited, as others did, conducting oneself as Kádár did in Hungary?
These questions remained open, although I did find answers to other
ones. For example, could we or could we not have done things in a
more cautious way, running less risk? Or on the other hand, would it
perhaps have been worthwhile to offer military resistance to military
intervention? To these and similar questions I answered in the negative,
but the main question remained unanswered: Was it worthwhile to
have begun this process at all? And should I myself have taken personal
responsibility for it?

In the end, on my own, I came to the following answer to my questions: I must always live in such a way as to feel myself to be a person
who shares the responsibility for what happens. One cannot avoid
responsibility by reference to good intentions, for as Dante long ago
observed, the road to hell is paved with them. In spite of that, I think
I simply could not have avoided taking part in the attempt to carry
through the Prague Spring. Because if out of fear of defeat I had done
nothing, I could not have justified myself to my own conscience, neither
as the confirmed Marxist I was at the time nor as the person I was with
the life story I had. Today I can justify myself to my conscience, but I
must of course admit that everyone else who did not have the possibility of choosing, nevertheless, had to pay for that experiment and
has the right to judge me differently than I do myself.

Today one often hears or reads unambiguous condemnations of
you, Misha. Not just in Western publications, where such things are
usually limited to assertions that Gorbachev failed or achieved the opposite of what he wanted. In your own country, in Russia, this takes
the form more usually of rude insults, tactless and one-sided allegations

that social, political, and governmental decline—and everything bad in general—"began under Gorbachev."

On the one hand, this is the "voice of the people" being expressed in an unjust way, the voice of people whose hopes were disappointed. On the other hand, it is the continuation of an earlier campaign against you and your policies by a number of your opponents. All of this is common enough in history, and I don't really want to talk about that aspect. My question is: How do you personally regard your own actions at the time when you were the chief representative and initiator of new Soviet policies domestically and internationally?

M.G.   To begin with, I'd like to say a few words about your problem in relation to 1968. I think you're quite right to draw the conclusion that despite its defeat the Prague Spring had its own meaning and significance. Because that defeat represented not just a new wave of repression against all attempts at democracy under "actually existing socialism," but from a dialectical point of view it also represented nothing less than the beginning of the end for the totalitarian system. So I think you should have a clear conscience on that score.

Naturally I feel troubled by the fact that I did not succeed in keeping the entire process of perestroika within the framework of my intentions, primarily within the framework of gradual but profound democratic change. I probably feel even more troubled than you did [over the Prague Spring] because my responsibility was greater, both on the scale of the Soviet Union and of world politics, and this responsibility increased the longer I remained at the head of the political leadership. Especially now, when I see that everything has been distorted and the reforms are heading in quite a different direction, it causes me great distress. But I suffer precisely over that, not because I actually began the struggle for democracy and fundamental change of the Soviet system. I do not regret that I began that struggle. It had to be done.

Now, with a certain distance from those events, I of course see many things differently, but in my fundamental positions nothing has changed: I would do it all over, and I would begin again with the struggle for "more democracy, more socialism." However, my understanding of socialism would now be different, and therefore I would approach the task in a more mature way. Because in 1985, and for some time after that, our desire was to improve, to make more socialist, a system that was not truly socialist. And the whole drama of our situation lay in that.

Today I would know that the goal had to be the removal of the totalitarian system, that reforms in all spheres of life—from monopoly ownership up to and including the ideological monopoly—would have to be more radical, more profound, more directed toward fundamental principles. But I would not abandon the basic choice I made—seeking to change what existed—and today I still think that was correct. Not only because it was necessary for the USSR, but because the rest of the world also needed it. And in that sense my conscience is also clear.

z.m   I understand your point completely. As far as perestroika is concerned, I think that although the present situation completely contradicts the aims you were pursuing in your policies, nevertheless a road was opened for new developments. What the final result will be only the future will show, but I consider the possibility of free development, which can no longer be suppressed by force, a positive thing in and of itself. That is also the case from the point of view of socialist ideas, because new possibilities for development were opened up for socialism as well. Paradoxically this includes the very fact that socialism is no longer equated with that system of "actually existing socialism."

m.g.   In regard to your last comment, I think that only history can provide an answer. But it is a big step forward that we are no longer trying to create ideal models and force the life of our society to fit into a preconceived mold. We have eliminated totalitarian governmental power, provided freedom of choice and democratic pluralism, and that is the main thing for the cause of socialism, which is inseparable from democracy.

z.m   One other question remains, Misha, one I encounter frequently and which also, of course, has to do with you. People sometimes ask this question: Don't you really see, even today, that the Soviet system could not have been reformed? It could only be destroyed. Its downfall is what should have happened, but that's exactly what you reform Communists did not want. Even today you don't understand that your main mistake was to hold the Communist convictions you did, and that those who wanted to crush and destroy Communism were always right.

I understand that, after everything that has happened, it is not only traditional anti-Communists of the Cold War era who think in such fashion, but many people who on the whole are quite tolerant, and this is especially true of the younger generation. In spite of this I think matters are much more complicated. After all, the lives the two of us have led, for example, serve as confirmation that within the Communist movement, within the framework of its ideology, it was not only possible but also logical that a desire for change should be born, a desire to fight for a human and democratic form of socialism. The contradiction between the original humanist content of Marxism and the totalitarian system of the Soviet type inevitably led to this result. This would not have been possible, incidentally, on the basis of fascist or Nazi ideology, although it is fashionable today to liken our Communist convictions to fascist ideology. What do you think about this problem?

M.G.   On the basis of my own experience, which is probably unique and hardly comparable to anyone else's, I am convinced that in the countries of "actually existing socialism" any attempts to begin reform and make change *from below* were doomed to failure. The system had the capacity to suppress such attempts and to effectively combat them. For that reason it was only possible and necessary to begin from the top down. And the fact that inside the USSR itself there appeared people who were seeking to make reforms, such as Khrushchev and, in the economic arena, Kosygin, and a few years later, to a certain limited extent, Andropov, then finally Gorbachev—all this shows that within the Soviet system, ideas and political aspirations could arise which, in the name of rejuvenating the system, were able to help overcome it.

Another question remains, however: Could the system have been reformed, or was it necessary to destroy it completely? I think there was a possibility of reform, but only on the basis of a radical approach to reform. That means an understanding that the totalitarian nature of power in the Soviet Union had to be overcome and eliminated, and that those elements in the system that tended to suppress freedom and make democratic decisions impossible had to be rejected. But this had to occur, not as an explosion of contradictions, but as reform with the aim of creating a qualitatively new system. What we are experiencing today is not that kind of reform; it is a reaction, an attempt to revive something out of the historical past. And I don't think it's accidental that it is from people in France, which has had the greatest experience with revolutions, as well as with restorations of old regimes, that I most frequently hear the warning: Don't go backwards, don't return to the past, seek your own way forward, seek a road that Russia has earned and paid for by its own experience.

Z.M   I think, then, that we are both agreed that we have nothing to be ashamed of in becoming reform Communists in our politics. We lost the possibility that we once had of influencing developments from positions of political power, but we did not lose our honor.

M.G.   Not only do we have nothing to be ashamed of. I think that, along with millions of others, we gave proof that in the Communist movement there were by no means just people who were hungry for power or seeking a career, but also unselfish people whose aspirations were in the direction of freedom and democracy.

Was There Betrayal? What Was Betrayed? By Whom? And When?

Z.M   The Communist reformers are criticized and attacked nowadays not only from the right but also from the "left." I put this word in quotation marks because various political currents are involved. The term includes outright supporters of the old system of the Stalinist type, that part of the bureaucracy, or *nomenklatura*, which was always opposed to perestroika. We also find people who consider themselves the "true left," but who would gladly return to the time before 1985 out of fear of the present unstable and risky course of development, because they still see great opportunities for socialism in the possibility, which has already been totally lost, of reforming "actually existing socialism"—they see greater opportunities in that than in the free development of society. In a way similar to representatives of conservative political currents in the West, they consider the present phase to be the "end of history," when in fact a great deal that should have been improved rather than destroyed perished along with the totalitarian relations in the old system. There is a big difference between Communists of this kind and the incorrigible Stalinists, even though they have one thing in common: they tend on the whole to rather lightly explain everything that happened as being a "betrayal of our ideals" on the part of those who began to fight to change the system; at the same time, they proclaim themselves to be the only "true fighters for the Communist cause."

For me this does not represent anything new. I have lived as a "betrayer" for more than a quarter of a century. But for that very reason I had to try to clarify for myself my own inner attitude toward the concepts of betrayal and loyalty to the ideals of Marxism, communism, and socialism. Because I cannot claim that I was not at all affected by such accusations at first. When I heard such accusations from officials of the government apparatus, who were well paid to promote the official line of Brezhnev's policies, that of course was a matter of indifference to me. But they were not the only ones who said such things. On the level of rational analysis I dealt with such charges by concluding that the Soviet system was above all a reactionary form of totalitarian power, as we have already discussed in detail. On the level of my subjective feelings I finally found the following answer for myself.

Changing one's views and convictions is not identical with betraying ideals. Besides, you can really only betray living human beings, not some sort of abstract cause of socialism or communism that has nothing to do with people.

Otherwise we would end up in the closed world of religious belief in such things as "manifest truth" or in the world of ideological and political sectarianism. Changing one's views and convictions is a completely necessary aspect of real life, because only the encounter between one's views and reality produces a result in which a person either remains with his or her original ideas or changes them.

I quite naturally was bound to arrive at some change in my views as a result of a conflict: my actual experiences in the years 1948–1968 clashed with my post-World War II hopes for the construction of a better, more just, and more rational world, and with the body of ideas I had accepted from Marx and, partly, from Lenin. I had to reexamine a great deal and change a great deal, but in the end I did so in keeping with my original beliefs and Marxist ideals and not in conflict with them. In regard to the people who I previously had tried to win over to the views which I myself later renounced, the problem was one solely of openness and sincerity. I never concealed the fact that my views had changed and never did anything secretly that contradicted what I was saying publicly. Consequently, I don't consider this a betrayal of the people who had placed confidence in me for many years. Those who did not share my change of views remained true to their own opinions, but I had neither deceived nor betrayed them. We had simply parted company as far as the views we held were concerned. In brief, then, regardless of who might accuse me of being a betrayer, my conscience is clear, and I do not feel that I have betrayed anyone or anything.

M.G.   Yes, I too feel that this is the heart of the matter. After all, the entire process of perestroika began and developed with both the party and society actively participating. There were plenary sessions of the CPSU Central Committee, one after the other, with more Central Committee plenary sessions being held (in six years) than during a decade of the Brezhnev era. Every decisive turn of events took place with the entire party participating, and it was all done absolutely openly. All my reports were approved by the Politburo, and I spoke publicly in the name of the Politburo. During all this there were debates and discussions, sometimes quite sharp ones, but that is a different question.

It also happened sometimes that participants in these debates would not speak to each other for several days afterward. But I never concealed my views or the way they developed and changed. And all of us together came to the conclusion that taking these forward steps on the road of perestroika was necessary and that these policies were beneficial to socialism.

When I was being held prisoner in the Crimea, in my vacation home at Foros, and when representatives of the makers of the August 1991 coup came to see me for the first time, I said to them openly: You assess the present situation as threatening, and it may be that I see it as even more threatening than you do. But the question is, How to proceed in seeking a way out of the situation? Using what methods? I am for the democratic way, implementing an anti-crisis economic program, signing a new Union Treaty, and democratically reforming the CPSU. You on the other hand propose emergency measures, martial law, and the use of force. To me that is unacceptable. But since such a conflict of opinion has arisen between us, let us immediately convene a Congress of People's Deputies and the Supreme Soviet. And let them decide. If they agree with your proposals, by all means let it be done your way. But for my part, I reject that and will not support it.

For me, betrayal in politics begins when legal and constitutional methods are trampled under foot and certain groups or individuals, using conspiratorial methods and relying on force, seek to have decisions carried out that they have made in secret. Disagreements and conflicts in politics of course can be completely principled; a policy disagreement can result in people resigning from their posts, let's say, as a sign of protest. If the makers of the August 1991 coup, instead of organizing their conspiracy, had openly declared that as a sign of protest and disagreement with the policies of Gorbachev they were submitting their resignations, they would have caused a governmental crisis, and the highest representative bodies of governmental power would then have had to resolve that crisis. In that case I would have had nothing to reproach them for. That is why to this day I regard [former Politburo member Igor] Ligachev's conduct in quite a different way. In principle he always spoke his views openly. While I did not agree with him, I never made any accusations against him, certainly not that of betrayal. I can say the same thing in regard to the former prime minister, Nikolai Ryzhkov.

z.m   I can confirm what you are saying, Misha, on the basis of my own experience after August 1968. I would only wish to add that there is also the question of the content of views that are publicly stated. In August 1968 I learned that some comrades in the leadership of the party openly held the view that I should be placed before a "revolutionary tribunal." I confess I was not ready to regard that as an expression of pluralism of opinion, even though people were expressing those views quite openly.

Yesterday in Moscow I met a man whose name I won't mention here. During the Brezhnev era he wrote critical essays about the administrative-command system of economic and governmental administration, and later on he was unquestionably a supporter of the policy of perestroika. I met with him several times during the perestroika era and respected him for his sober and serious approach to the question of changing the system, something we both considered necessary. Today, in contrast, he belongs to the ranks of the "healthy nucleus" of Communists who consider even Gennady Zyuganov (leader of the Communist Party of the Russian Federation), strictly speaking, to be on the right. When I told him I was coming to see you today he spoke quite candidly: "Don't be offended. I know that's he's your friend, but it was my duty to write about him that he was a Yudushka [a term insinuating "Judas," but actually derived from the character Yudushka Golovlyov in the novel *The Golovlyov Family* by the nineteenth-century Russian satirist Saltykov-Shchedrin] and a betrayer." I asked him: "What did he betray? And when and how?" He answered: "Well, after all, everything that has come about as a result of his policies is objectively a betrayal of socialism." He was trained in a law school just as you and I were, and so I was truly surprised that he connected the terms "objectively" and "betrayal."

m.g.   Vyshinsky would have been overjoyed to hear that!

z.m   That's what I told him. I said the Soviet Academy of Sciences should restore the old name to one of its institutes—the Vyshinsky Institute of State and Law. Because Vyshinsky, the chief prosecutor in Stalin's show trials, was also the chief proponent of the absurd principle that you can commit treason without being subjectively guilty, without conscious intent. I gave him an example: "If during a war the commander of a front or even the commander-in-chief of the army loses a decisive battle, and even if he made fatal errors contributing to the defeat, can you really call him a traitor?" He replied that if he made those mistakes in an effort to save his own skin, then yes, it was betrayal. To that I responded with another question: "When did Gorbachev try to save his own skin?" After all, losing a battle is not the same thing as treason. He finally began to hesitate at that point and said he would think about it further. I told him that I had already been thinking about it for a quarter of a century, because during all that time I had been hearing from various "true believers" that I myself was a traitor. That was the reason, I said, why I could not think of Gorbachev as a betrayer, not just because I was a friend of his.

I think there are many Communists who hold such views to this day, confusing adherence to principle with simple stubbornness. Their idea of loyalty to ideals is the equivalent of refusing to pay attention to actual results in the test of life itself. It's interesting to notice in all this that they don't accuse Stalin and his followers of betrayal but only the reform Communists who sought to change the Stalinist system. The only thing they have to say about the Stalin era is that they didn't know about the crimes or, let's say, that they reached the age of maturity only after all that was over. But by this they are admitting, strictly speaking, that Stalin succeeded in deceiving them. What he did in fact was different from what he proclaimed and what they thought he was doing. But that doesn't bother them at all, even though that constituted the very essence of betrayal—betrayal of those who believed he was a great "leader and teacher."

m.g.   Complex and contradictory situations sometimes arise this way. On the one hand, I respect people who openly say they have not changed their views because, unlike us, they have found no reason to. This is a position that is entirely possible to take within the framework of pluralism. On the other hand, a person who refuses to change his or her views simply out of stubbornness is taking a typical sectarian stand, and sectarians are usually inclined, in the name of "principle," to head in an antidemocratic direction. My experience has taught me one other thing: many representatives of the old *nomenklatura* talk about the "betrayal of socialism," but in fact they are not at all concerned about the ideals of communism or the fate of socialism; they are only pursuing their selfish interests, the old privileges and high positions they enjoyed as part of the *nomenklatura*. At the same time it was precisely from the ranks of such people that the real deceivers and traitors emerged, people who behind the backs of everyone else were preparing an attempt at a coup d'etat with the use of force, while outwardly behaving as though they were supporters of perestroika. It is these same kind of people who today are grabbing formerly publicly owned property as their own private property, and on an enormous scale at that, exploiting people and forgetting their former incantations about socialism.

To finish what we are saying on the subject of betrayal, let me describe the following incident. During my travels in Siberia [during perestroika] when I was speaking at one of the universities a certain instructor carrying a large briefcase stood up before an overflow crowd in an assembly hall at the university and asked if he could pose a question to me. He was given the floor, and he then began to read various statements I had made at various times during the perestroika era. They constituted proof that I had changed my views. Then came the "treacherous" question (and from the point of view of this instructor it was a devastating question): "So then, what are you really? After all, in political language, this is nothing other than betrayal." I answered that when Lenin introduced the New Economic Policy (NEP), many people also called him a betrayer in exactly the same way, saying that he had sold out to the bourgeoisie. Some people even committed suicide [in protest against the NEP]. In the last articles he wrote, analyzing the path the revolution had taken since 1917, Lenin came to the conclusion that a radical change in our point of view toward socialism was necessary. "Why," I asked, "do you defend Lenin's right to change his views and deny me that same right?" A big burst of applause filled the room.

Revealing the Secrets of Rooms "Behind Closed Doors"

Z.M.   Yes, that is a powerful answer and right to the point. To conclude our conversations, I would like to return to a subject that people have often found interesting. One close acquaintance of mine put it concisely, as follows: "No matter what you say, you are a man who has been behind those sound-proofed, padded doors where approximately a dozen people decide the fate of everyone else." This applies to you too, Misha, to an incomparably greater extent: you were number one among those who made the decisions, and you were in that position for six years, not six months, and the destinies, not just of one small country but of the whole world, were being decided. People are definitely interested in knowing what a person feels who has been in such a secret room "behind closed doors," not accessible to others and mysterious in its own way. How does such a person feel when they have returned to normal, everyday life? I can sum up my own brief experience in that regard by making three points.

First, I know that, in and of itself, power at the very top is much more limited and can accomplish significantly less than I imagined before I went behind those closed doors. Second, I know those doors seal off the occupants of the room not only from noise, from the human voices and sounds of the outer world that cannot penetrate those sound-proofed doors, but to the same degree those doors isolate the people that go behind them from the rest of the world and from life itself. The very short time I spent behind the "closed doors" of power contributed something quite useful to me: I lost the desire that almost any political person is bound to have, the desire to be there among the people who have the right of admission, the right to go behind the closed doors. Whoever has been in that position once should not necessarily rule out the possibility that he could return there again, but he no longer feels it as an urgent need, but rather as a condition for accomplishing his goals. But this is only true if the person is striving toward something different, not for the sake of power itself, if power for such a person is only a means and not an end in itself. What are your feelings in this connection?

M.G. I feel a great kinship with the thoughts you have expressed, Zdeněk, most likely because you and I are very close in spirit. It is not an accident that we met and became friends in our youth without having any ulterior aims, not calculating any sort of advantage from that friendship. And our friendship has lasted for decades, surviving every ordeal. I would like to add two comments to what you have said. I think that indeed a big part is played by the question of whether a person conceives of power as some sort of supreme value, as a goal in itself. For me power never had that kind of meaning . . .

Z.M I'm glad to hear that, because that's literally what I wrote in my first article about you, in the Italian Communist newspaper *Unita,* immediately after you rose to the position of general secretary of the CPSU. I wrote that, for Gorbachev, power is only a means, but the aim of politics is to change and improve people's lives.

M.G. I know that. I read your article at the time. But it's precisely for that reason that my withdrawal from political power is bound up with many painful feelings; it is painful that I didn't succeed in keeping the whole process on track in the direction I wanted it to go. Today the position I am in is unique . . .

Z.M Yes, a private individual with international standing and, in general, the status of a retired statesman.

M.G. Something like that. I now have a special privilege—to think without the limitations imposed by the feeling of responsibility one has when occupying a high governmental position.

On the whole, I agree with you that a person at the heights of power comes to see that he still can't achieve everything he thought possible. At first I thought when I moved from Stavropol to Moscow things would change. But when I was a secretary of the Central Committee and then a member of the Politburo, I still had to argue about certain things, now with Kosygin and Kirilenko, now with Tikhonov and Chernenko. I would try to prove my point, argue the truth as I saw it, but often without success. And when I became general secretary I had to pay attention to the overall circumstances, to the consequences of any steps I took, and to the opinions of the other members of the leadership.

When I was already in the top post I had to answer the question several times of how I would feel if I had to leave that post because I might not be reelected to it. During a state visit I made to Japan a student asked me directly about that during a television interview. I said that it would be a natural consequence of democracy, that I would consider being replaced through democratic elections a victory for my policy of perestroika, because no such thing had ever happened before in the USSR. We had only one tradition—you left the Kremlin surrounded with flowers to take your place either in the Lenin Mausoleum or at least in the wall of the Kremlin [where many former leaders are buried].

z.m   But there were also worse cases, when there were no flowers, and people were put against an entirely different kind of wall.

m.g.   Yes, there was that variation during the Stalin era. So a new kind of precedent began with me, although things still aren't proceeding in the best way.

z.m   On the other hand, Khrushchev left power in a way that, considering the Soviet tradition, was more or less normal. He went into retirement and received a pension.

m.g.   In a certain sense, yes, but at the price of remaining silent. I am not about to remain silent, although some people would very much like me to do so. I am sometimes asked the question, "Do I want to return to active politics?" My answer is as follows: in the political sky there are many stars of various magnitudes, in different locations, and giving off different kinds of light. There is also room there for my star. I am not about to go off and live in the taiga; I remain in politics.

z.m   I have also had occasion several times to answer the question of whether I would return to politics. My answer is that I have never left politics. I don't hold any political posts or public offices, and I have no aspirations in that direction. But I think that a person, by the views he expresses and the particular positions he takes, can have a presence in politics and exert a certain influence on people. A person has not disappeared from politics just because he holds no posts or has become undesirable or inconvenient for those who do hold power, even if he has become an object of slander and political attack. A person disappears from politics only if people are indifferent to him, and I don't think that is the case for me, and even less so for you. Each of us "intervenes" in politics in his own way, and I think we will be heard loud and clear in the future as well.

m.g.   To that I would only like to add that we not only have the right to be in politics but that, strictly speaking, it is our moral responsibility. And I think we do have something to say.

z.m   It is possible that some of the things we have to say will be of more interest to people in our countries—in the Czech Republic and in Russia—and of more interest tomorrow than today. But let today's and tomorrow's readers be the judge of that. In any case, I can say for myself that I did not win politically in the main battles I fought, but it does not seem to me that I lost either. It can't be said that I'm happy about it, but I would not complain in any way about the life I've lived; I don't consider it to have been either empty or useless.

m.g.   Some time ago, Zdeněk, I wrote that fate willed that I be given a task of a kind that very rarely falls to the lot of a single human being.

At the same time it was a burden that was so heavy that only my closest friends know how hard things were for me sometimes, and still can be to this day, to the point of despair. But I accept it as fate: there are no happy reformers.